THE UNMARRIED MOTHER
IN GERMAN LITERATURE

THE UNMARRIED MOTHER
IN GERMAN LITERATURE

WITH SPECIAL REFERENCE TO THE
PERIOD 1770–1800

BY

OSCAR HELMUTH WERNER

SUBMITTED IN PARTIAL FULFILMENT OF THE REQUIREMENTS
FOR THE DEGREE OF DOCTOR OF PHILOSOPHY, IN THE
FACULTY OF PHILOSOPHY, COLUMBIA UNIVERSITY

New York
COLUMBIA UNIVERSITY PRESS
1917

Approved for publication on behalf of the Department of Germanic Languages and Literatures of Columbia University.

CALVIN THOMAS.

NEW YORK; May 1, 1917

PREFACE

That the problem of unmarried motherhood plays an important rôle in the life of the nations of the Occident is proved conclusively by the fact that before the present war there were born in Germany 177,000 illegitimate children annually, in France 80,000, in England 38,000, in Sweden 18,000, in little Norway 5,000. In the cities of the United States about 3 per cent of all births are illegitimate, which is low as compared with European countries. The extent of the divorce evil in our country counterbalances this, for out of every twelve marriages contracted one ends in divorce. It is no wonder, therefore, that the nations of the Occident have in the last decade been actively engaged in an attempt to solve this problem of unmarried motherhood. In Germany and the Scandinavian countries a widespread movement called "Mutterschutz" has lately sought reforms in the laws of the state and in the opinions of society to the end of removing the disgrace which attaches to the illegitimate child and its mother. In 1913 France finally abolished the famous Napoleonic edict: "La recherche de la paternité est interdite." In 1914 Austria followed with the abolition of an equally notorious law whereby "illegitimate children were excluded from family and relationship rights." The Norwegian Storthing in 1915 passed a "law concerning children whose parents have not married," whose intention is to give every child two parents. And in our country the Department of Labor has recently undertaken "a study into the problems presented by the unmarried mothers of America," which is to be "the most elaborate inquiry of its kind ever attempted by the federal government."

The dynamic behind this movement is the realization that the unmarried mother and her child are victims of circumstances for which they are generally not responsible and that therefore the stigma which a former civilization has attached to them is unjust. Modern civilization no longer accepts the

vii

rule of the ancients that woman is "the gate of the devil," but it insists that the sanctity of all motherhood can best be restored to society by the acceptance of the principle that man and not woman is the aggressor in sex matters, all examples to the contrary being pitiful perversions of nature which were probably brought into existence involuntarily.

But this dissertation was undertaken primarily to find, if possible, a more satisfactory explanation than has been given hitherto for Goethe's utilization of the theme of unmarried motherhood with its consequent infanticide in his "Faust." It was suggested by Professor Calvin Thomas that a study of the laws and customs contemporary with Goethe might throw light upon this question. The investigation was not limited, therefore, to the field of belles lettres but included all literature of the period which might have a bearing on the subject. In the first two chapters I have accordingly devoted much space to a discussion of all literature on the subject up to 1800, devoting Chapter III more particularly to the belles lettres of the Storm and Stress period. The original intention of adding a chapter on the development of the problem in German life and literature from 1800 to the present time was not carried out because of its unsuspected extent. A study of this period with especial reference to the changed attitude of the church shall be the subject of a future research.

I cannot express properly in words my gratefulness to Professor Calvin Thomas for his infinite patience and constant encouragement in the preparation of this dissertation, as well as for his advice and help in many other ways. I am also indebted to Professor Arthur F. J. Remy for the encouragement in the prosecution of my studies in the German saga world, to Professor W. Addison Hervey and Dr. Traugott Böhme for their interest in my research and valuable suggestions relating to it, and to Professor Frederick W. J. Heuser for his criticism. I wish also to express my gratitude to my colleague, Mr. W. D. Trautmann, for suggestions and assistance in the reading of the proof.

CLEVELAND, April 12, 1917.

CONTENTS

Popularity of theme of unmarried motherhood during Storm and Stress period, 1. In imaginative literature, 2. In non-imaginative literature, 3. The Mannheim prize, 4. Source of extensive literature, 6. Extent of infanticide in real life, 7. The present problem, 11.

CHAPTER I

Marriage among primitive peoples, 12. Legal marriage, 14. Celibacy vs. marriage in early Christian church, 15. Conflict of church with concubinage, 17. With legal infanticide, 18. Theories of punishment applied to illegitimate sex relations, 23. Theory of revenge, 23. Theory of betterment, 24. "Abschreckungstheorie," 24. Illegitimate infanticide, 25. Punishments inflicted on unmarried mothers in Middle Ages, 26. Sacking, 26. Burying alive, 26. Empalement, 27. Public church penance, 27. Carolina, 29. Failure of "Abschreckungstheorie," 32. First traces of revolt, 34. Frederick the Great, 34. Contemporary rulers, 37. Beccaria, 38.

CHAPTER II

Causes of wide-spread illegitimacy in last half of eighteenth century, 40. Inflated prosperity, 41. Emigration from country to city, 42. Social gatherings conducive to immorality, 43. Literature, 44. Hosts of unmarried, 46. Soldiers, 46. Soldier-marriages, 48. Nobility, 52. Revolt against antiquated laws, 56. Natural law vs. social law, 56. Capital punishment, 58. Torture, 60. Revolt against canon law, 61. Public church penance, 62. Punishment of seducer, 65. Foundling-houses, 67.

CHAPTER III

Universality of the tragedy of unmarried motherhood, 69.
Personal experience of the writers as a source of productions, 69.
Didacticism, 70. Seduction, 74. Infanticide, 76. Differentiation of voluntary and involuntary unmarried motherhood, 80.
Motives which prompted infanticide, 82. Desertion, 82. The
forsaken girl, 82. Hatred, 86. Jealousy of another girl, 87.
Fear of shame, 88. Ridicule of parents, 88. The blustering
father, 88. Ridicule of the world, 90. Dark outlook for future
of child, 92. Emphasis by church on virginity at marriage, 93.
Despair, 95. Superstition, 96. The hell-motif, 100. The
eternal feminine, 102.

CHAPTER IV

Results of the agitation, 105. Contribution of writers through
personal efforts, 107. Effectiveness of non-esthetic literature,
108. The two-fold aim of imaginative literature, 108. Influence
on public opinion, 109. Value as esthetic literature, 109.

INTRODUCTION

In October, 1853, a reader of the *Anzeiger für Kunde der deutschen Vorzeit* asked the following questions: "Goethe in his 'Faust' lets the offended brother of the unfortunate Gretchen imprecate all kinds of punishments for her mistake, or rather recounts them as presupposed results. Did the poet . . . invent these punishments and social detriments which Gretchen was to experience? Did he draw from folk-tradition or from historical sources? Where in fact does one find authentic reports about the punishments of unchastity in the Middle Ages, and especially about the punishments inflicted on fallen girls by church and society?" Twenty years later another student of Goethe asked: "How did it come that in spite of the free sexual relations among the lower classes and in spite of the tremendous power of the sexual impulse, cases like Gretchen's were comparatively rare, so that every time such a sexual lapse resulted in infanticide it caused the greatest ado and horror?"[1]

Both inquirers presupposed what we know to be a fact, namely, that the source of Goethe's poetic creations was real life. They did not know that the unmarried mother, who usually killed her new-born child, was the most popular literary theme of the Storm and Stress epoch, or that infanticide was the most common crime in western Europe from the Middle Ages to the end of the eighteenth century.

Erich Schmidt, as early as 1875, pointed out that "the theme of infanticide as a continuation of the theme of seduction haunts many writers" of the Storm and Stress period.[2] In his introduction to a reprint of Wagner's "Die Kindermörderinn" he refers again to the theme, "which was so

---

[1] Reinhard Röpe, "Gretchens Schuld," 1873. A chapter in his "Unbewusste Zeugnisse für die christliche Wahrheit." Hamburg, 1877. p. 127.

[2] In his "Heinrich Leopold Wagner. Goethes Jugendgenosse." Jena, 1879. p. 98.

1

popular in drama, prose narrative and juridical literature."[3] In spite of Max Koch's assertion that the theme was one "which all poets of this youthful school attempted to utilize,"[4] scholars generally refer to its use by a few writers only. Thus Eduard Engel says: "Infanticide and punishment of the murderess were among the frequently treated subjects: Bürger, Lenz, Maler Müller, later Schiller and even Goethe treated it, as did H. L. Wagner with crude realism."[5] Karl Credner in the introduction to an excellent collection of extracts from the literature of the Storm and Stress is right in his assertion that "the infanticide is a typical figure of the Storm and Stress from Goethe to Schiller and exceeds in frequency even the favored pair of hostile brothers."[6]

Gräf,[7] in recording Goethe's famous statement regarding Wagner's so-called plagiarism, calls attention to a letter of Goethe to Zelter in which he wrote: "All the foolishness about pre- and postoccupation, about plagiarism and partial theft is perfectly clear to me and in my opinion silly. For what is in the air and what the time demands can originate in a hundred heads at the same time without the necessity of borrowing, one from another." Probably Gräf was right in suggesting that Goethe was thinking particularly of the popularity of the theme of infanticide, for we have an interesting parallel to Goethe's statement in a foot-note to August Gott-

---

[3] P. iii in No. 13 of "Deutsche Litteraturdenkmale des 18. und 19. Jahrhunderts." Heilbronn, 1883.

[4] "Helferich Peter Sturz." München, 1879, p. 211.

[5] "Geschichte der deutschen Literatur." Leipzig und Wien, 1907, II, 577.

[6] Introduction, p. 11, to "Voigtländers Quellenbücher. No. 70. Sturm und Drang. Quellenstücke zur literarischen Revolution der Originalgenies." Leipzig, 1915. Other evidence for the popularity of the theme may be found in Richard Weltrich, "Friedrich Schiller." Stuttgart, 1899, p. 532; "Stürmer und Dränger." Hrsg. von August Sauer, I, 45f.; Cäsar Flaischlen, "Otto Heinrich Freiherr von Gemmingen. Mit einer Vorstudie über Diderot," Stuttgart, 1890, p. 122; Georg Joseph Pfeiffer, "Klinger's Faust," Würzburg, 1887, p. 13f.; Konstantin Muskalla, "Johann Timotheus Hermes," Breslau, 1910, p. 27f.; Theodor Mertens, "Die Kerkerscene aus Goethes Faust," Hannover, 1873, p. 34; etc.

[7] Hans Gerhard Gräf: "Goethe über seine Dichtungen." Frankfurt am Main, 1904, IV, 206. The letter to Zelter is in "Briefe" XXVII, 220.

lieb Meissner's poem "Die Mörderin."[8]   Meissner, referring
to the similarity of his poem with another by Anton Matthias
Sprickmann entitled "Ida," says: "I know very well, that
several parts of 'Ida' in the February number of the *Museum*
for 1777 are similar to this poem, but as an honest man I can
affirm that the poem was finished several months before I even
saw that one.   A new example of how often two heads think
of the same thing without borrowing anything from each
other."

When Boie suggested to Bürger that he should read Wagner's play the latter answered: "Wagner's 'Die Kindermörderinn' I have not seen as yet.   The title, however, strikes me
because I have carried a dramatic subject by the same title
around with me for a long time.   I wish Wagner's production
were poor.   Lenz too recently crossed my plans with 'Die
Soldaten,' in which he depicted many a situation as if he had
copied them right out of my soul."[9]   To this Boie answered in
a letter which is a remarkable index to the popularity of the
theme: "Wagner's 'Die Kindermörderinn' as well as Lenz's
'Die Soldaten' can be excelled and should not frighten you.
. . . . Sprickmann has composed an 'Infanticide' also. . . . .
How is it about your projected ballad 'Die Kindermörderin'?
I should like to read something dramatic by you.   If you do
not come out with yours soon, it will become more and more
difficult."[10]

The extensive utilization of the theme of infanticide by the
writers of this period was paralleled by a much more extensive
discussion of the crime in literature other than imaginative.
Wainlud in a recent monograph asserts that infanticide and
its prevention was the favorite theme of the criminologists of
that time.[11]   Rothenberger calls attention to the wide discussion of means to care for the poor, to the evil effects of

[8] Meissner's two poems "Lied einer Gefallenen" and "Die Mörderin" were
published in *Deutsches Museum*, 1779[1], p. 379ff.   Sprickmann's "Ida" is in
Deutsches Museum, 1777[1], p. 120ff.

[9] Cf. " Briefe von und an Gottfried August Bürger."   Hrsg. von Adolf Strodtmann.   Berlin, 1874, letter of Sept. 15, 1776.

[10] Cf. *idem*, letter of Sept. 27, 1776.

[11] Samuel Wainlud, "Die Kindstötung."   Berlin, 1905, p. 22.

luxury, and then to a "förmliche Kindermordlitteratur."[12] Seyffarth, the editor of the best edition of Pestalozzi's works, says: "The question how infanticide might be stopped was at that time a burning one."[13]

The great interest in infanticide can best be brought to view by the contest for a prize of 100 ducats offered by von Dalberg, intendant of the Mannheim theater, for the best essay on the subject: "What are the best and most practicable means to eradicate infanticide without promoting prostitution?" The contest closed at Whitsuntide, 1781. The offer of the prize was published in most of the newspapers and magazines of that time and was generally accompanied by editorial comments. The editorial in August Ludwig Schlözer's magazine *Briefwechsel* is typical. "There are crimes committed among us," the editor writes, "which are the most horrible and at the same time the most common, and among these is infanticide; crimes which are related to virtues, virtues which develop into vices, and among these too is infanticide; crimes which experience teaches are not made less frequent by increasing the severity of the punishment, while not to punish them would bring disgrace to mankind and destruction to law and order, and among these too is infanticide. . . . How long shall we lead to the block these unfortunate girls as sacrificial victims, whose love and the natural weakness of their sex, whose adornment of innocence and modesty has made them to be mothers and murderesses?"[14]

The number of essays submitted for the prize is said to have been four hundred, which was an unusually large number for that time. It is no wonder that a contributor to Schlözer's magazine suggested: "The prize question, how infanticide might be checked, has alarmed so many scholars in all the faculties that one is amazed at the large number of essays submitted. I should not like to be one of those appointed to

---

[12] Christian Rothenberger, "Pestalozzi als Philosoph." Bern, 1898. See "Berner Studien zur Philosophie und ihrer Geschichte," XI, 27.

[13] "Pestalozzi's sämtliche Werke." Hrsg. von L. W. Seyffarth. Liegnitz, 1900, V, 345. Cf. also Karl Berger, "Schiller, sein Leben und seine Werke." München, 1906, p. 215.

[14] *Briefwechsel*, VII, 261ff.

judge the multitude of answers; I believe I should be bored to death."[15] A writer in the *Allgemeine Deutsche Bibliothek* expresses similar astonishment.[16]

Three essays won the prize, each of the three judges awarding it to a different contestant. The winners were Pfeil, Klippstein,[17] and Kreuzfeld;[18] the judges the coadjutor von Dalberg (Erfurt), Michaelis (Göttingen) and Rigal (Mannheim). In addition to these three, a large number of the other essays submitted were published. More than three dozen of them were reviewed in the *Allgemeine Deutsche Bibliothek*. The most interesting and to my mind the most important of them all was an essay by Pestalozzi,[19] which was not submitted to the judges. The reason is found in a letter to Isaak Iselin, in which the great educator wrote: "I hope it will not displease you, but I do not intend to submit it as a prize-essay, but instead, if possible, to sell it to a publisher in Basel, in order that it may be published by Easter. I believe the subject-matter is of such general interest that it would be a good article for the book-stores."[20] Pestalozzi did not find a publisher immediately, however, and therefore printed parts of the essay in the *Schweizer-Blatt* which he edited during the one year of its existence in 1782.

Another essay written but not submitted for the prize was that by Ludwig von Hess, who although a German was Councillor to the Swedish government at this time. Instead of submitting the essay he published it immediately, in order that he "might perhaps prevent one more infanticide."[21]

---

[15] *Briefwechsel*, X, 352f.

[16] 57, 142.

[17] Not Klingenstein, as Erich Schmidt has it in his "Heinrich Leopold Wagner. Goethes Jugendgenosse," p. 92.

[18] The three essays were published together in book form in 1784 (not 1785. Cf. Erich Schmidt, "Heinrich Leopold Wagner," p. 92) by Schwan in Mannheim under the title: "Drei Preisschriften über die Frage: Welches sind die besten ausführbarsten Mittel dem Kindermorde abzuhelfen, ohne die Unzucht zu begünstigen?"

[19] The essay was entitled: Ueber Gesetzgebung und Kindermord. Wahrheiten und Träume. Nachforschungen und Bilder. Vom Verfasser Lienhards und Gertrud. Geschrieben 1780. Herausgegeben 1783. Frankfurt und Leipzig.

[20] From a letter dated Feb. 13, 1781. "Sämtliche Werke," I, 227.

[21] Cf. *Allgemeine Deutsche Bibliothek*, 48, 96.

The reviews of the published essays in the *Allgemeine Deutsche Bibliothek* are of particular interest because they generally rejected the remedies proposed. When the last essays were being published one of the reviewers remarked that most of the answers were "in part impracticable and nonsensical projects of government, in part dangerous quackery, in part insufficient palliatives."[22]

This extensive discussion of infanticide in editorials and in these essays was preceded by the publication of similar discussions for thirty years. Frederick the Great had been concerned with the problem since the year of his coronation.[23] Justus Möser, perhaps the most eminent and at the same time the most conservative jurist of that time, had attacked the problem in a number of smaller essays, the most important of which was "Ueber die zu unsern Zeiten verminderte Schande der Huren und Hurkinder."[24] Isaak Iselin had written an article "Gedanken über den Kindermord."[25]

The assertion that the literature on the subject came entirely from the camp of the "philanthropists" is untenable, for infanticide was of interest to every school of thought and to men of every profession, to old and young, to the learned and the unlearned. There was Pestalozzi, the educator, Iselin and Schlözer, the publicists, Möser, the jurist, Kant, the philosopher, Pfeil, the physician, Klippstein, the city official, Kreuzfeld, the professor, J. G. Schlosser, the overseer of an orphan asylum, Barkhausen, the lawyer, Herder, the preacher, Bürger, Goethe and Schiller, the poets, and scores of others who talked of and wrote on the subject. It is important to remember that the discussion of infanticide was not limited to a few "stormy" youths called "original geniuses," but that sagacious men of every calling devoted a part of their best effort to an attempt to solve this problem.

Goethe himself was indeed a typical representative of this period in portraying the fate of Gretchen. For the infanticide

[22] *Ibid.,* 54, 176.
[23] Cf. *infra,* p. 35.
[24] Cf. "Justus Möser's sämmtliche Werke." Berlin und Stettin, 1798, II, 163ff.
[25] In *Ephemeriden der Menschheit,* 1778. Viertes Stück. Cf. also *Allgemeine Deutsche Bibliothek,* 39, 593f.

had the sympathy of every believer in the inherent goodness of human nature. It was she, more than any other criminal, who had been forced by circumstances to do what she did not wish to do. And the number of those who were compelled to commit the crime was by no means small. Pestalozzi tells how he felt when he heard that infanticide was possible: "Infanticide! Do I dream or am I awake! Is it possible, this deed? Does it happen? Does the unnamed happen? No, not the unnamed, the named, the crime which has found expression in words. Conceal thy face, O Century! Bow down, O Europe! From the seats of justice comes the answer: my children are killed by the thousands at the hands of those who give birth to them. . . . In vain runs the blood of thy infanticides, O Europe! Let thy rulers remove the causes of their despair, and thou wilt save their children. Thy sword has killed many an infanticide during my time, but I shall tell the story of the first one only!"[26]

In one chapter of his discourse Pestalozzi includes fifteen cases of infanticide which he took from the records of the archives of Neuhof. Heinrich Leopold Wagner in a defence of his drama "Die Kindermörderinn" said: "There is no kind of crime of which our century has not one or more examples; regicides have been quartered, patricides and fratricides have been broken on the wheel, infanticides without number have been decapitated."[27] Georg Dietrich List in his Mannheim essay recounts the causes of this crime and then concludes: "Is it any wonder, then, that infanticide—for so sad experience teaches—is in our days becoming more and more frequent?"[28] Schlözer tells of old women who made it a business to take new-born illegitimate children to foundling houses, the tax for such a "service of love" being a half louis d'or.[29] The estates of Weimar and Eisenach in 1763 petitioned Duchess Anna Amalia to abolish public church penance because it was largely responsible "for the frequently occurring

[26] In the above-mentioned essay, p. 434.

[27] Cf. Erich Schmidt, "Heinrich Leopold Wagner, Goethes Jugendgenosse." Jena, 1879, p. 97.

[28] In his essay "Ueber Hurerey und Kindermord." Mannheim, 1784, p. 10.

[29] *Briefwechsel*, VII, 150.

infanticide."[30]   Johann Froitzheim asserts more recently that
"the number of girls executed for infanticide in Strassburg was
very large, especially before the erection of the foundling house
by prefect Klinglin in 1749."[31]   Pastor Niederer of Sennwald,
in a letter to Pestalozzi under date of August 11, 1800, com-
plained: "I am discovering daily from examples which occur
in my own congregation the horrifying extent of infanticide
and the innumerable prejudices and circumstances which
multiply it."   And Möser reports the examination of 785
cases of illegitimate sex relations on the part of young girls,
in order to find out, if possible, what types of girls usually
committed infanticide."[32]

 Corroboration of these statements can be found in the
archives of every imperial city of Europe.[33]   It is not necessary to recount here what these records reveal, nor is it worth
while to attempt to connect every individual literary production on the subject with some specific case in real life, as
Froitzheim tried to do with Goethe's "Faust," Wagner's
"Die Kindermörderinn," and Lenz's "Die Soldaten."[34]   The
fact is that infanticide was so common in the last half of the
eighteenth century that unless a specific case is mentioned by
the writer himself, or by his immediate friends, no one case
can be looked upon as the sole source of any particular literary
production.   Frederick the Great could write to Voltaire

[30] Cf. Bernhard Suphan "Goethe im Conseil," in *Vierteljahrschrift für
Litteraturgeschichte.* Weimar, 1893, VI, 604.

[31] In his "Goethe und Heinrich Leopold Wagner." Strassburg, 1889, p. 59.

[32] Justus Möser, "Patriotische Phantasien," in "Sämmtliche Werke."
Berlin, 1843, V, 108.

[33] For a record of cases of infanticide in real life during the last half of the
eighteenth century see Karl Goedeke, "Gottfried August Bürger in Göttingen
und Gelliehausen." Hannover, 1873, pp. 83-93; Theodor Gottlieb Hippel,
"Nachricht die von K*sche Untersuchung betreffend" in "Sämmtliche Werke,"
XI, 247ff.; Kreuzfeld in his essay, pp. 111, 129; "Der neue Pitaval. Eine
Sammlung der interessantesten Criminalgeschichten aller Länder aus älterer
und neuerer Zeit." Leipzig, 1857-1890, II, 401ff. IV, 276ff. XXIX.; *Archiv
des Criminalrechts,* Halle, 1798-1849, II, Art. 13, III, Art. 6; C. Spielmann,
"Kindesmord und seine Bestrafung im 17ten Jahrhunderte," in *Nassovia:
Zeitschrift für nassauische Geschichte und Heimatkunde.* Wiesbaden, XIII,
249ff.; see the same magazine, IX, 146ff.; etc.

[34] In his "Goethe und Heinrich Leopold Wagner. Ein Wort der Kritik an
unsere Goethe-Forscher." Strassburg, 1889, p. 45ff.

in 1777[35] that "of the criminals executed the most were girls who killed their infants, few were murderers and still fewer highway robbers," and specifically stated that the number of these criminals was from fourteen to fifteen annually. When we remember that because of his efforts for more than three decades to solve the problem of unmarried motherhood the number of those who committed infanticide in Prussia must have been few in comparison with the rest of western Europe, where all the old laws and customs were driving unmarried mothers to infanticide, and consequently in western Europe the number of these hapless creatures must have been over a hundred annually, it is not necessary to search the archives of any particular city to find a single case of infanticide which might have inspired three "stormy" youths to write dramas on the same subject.

Suffice it to refer to two cases of infanticide which occurred in the early eighties of the eighteenth century, right in the middle of the period of the Storm and Stress. The one is that of Katherine Elisabeth Erdmann of Benniehausen, who was tried in 1781 in a court in which Bürger sat as presiding judge. Her trial revealed that she was in every sense an actual infanticide, her illegitimate child having cried before she killed it.[36] Because of the excellent conduct of the trial by Bürger, however, she was not sentenced to death. Schlözer in reviewing another case suggested that it was the attorney for the defence, a Mr. Erxleben, who should be credited for this. Professor Justus Claproth thought differently. As a lecturer in the faculty of law in the University of Göttingen he thought so

[35] Cf. "Oeuvres de Frédéric le Grand." Berlin, 1853, XXIII, 461f. letter of Oct. 11, 1777.

[36] Ever since the publication of the first code of criminal law by Charles V (cf. *infra*, p. 29) great stress had been laid on the question: Was the child born alive or was it dead at birth? Jurists decided that a child had been killed intentionally if it lived at birth. The usual methods for determining whether a child lived at birth were: (a) The lung test. The lungs of the dead child were placed in water: if they swam, they contained air and the child had breathed, consequently had been killed. (b) The navel cord test. If the navel cord was tied when the child was found there was evidently no intent to kill, if the cord was not tied, there certainly was intent. (c) The blue mark test. The body of the dead child was carefully examined for blue marks. If some were found force had been used and there was intentional infanticide.

highly of the conduct of the case by Bürger that he published a digest, fifty pages in length, and thereafter used it in his classroom as a model for his students.[37]

The case of Margarethe Kölblinn forms a striking contrast to that presided over by Bürger. This unfortunate girl, who had given birth to a dead child, in 1783 in the Upper Palatinate became the victim of judicial arbitrariness.[38] She was a girl of the peasant class, had ignorantly concealed her pregnancy and later the child-birth, but the child was found, and she was arrested and brought to trial for intentional infanticide. At the trial she confessed giving birth to a dead illegitimate child, but the court refused to accept her testimony and proceeded with the usual tests. It was found that she had failed to do anything to make conviction on the tests impossible, evidently because of ignorance, and she was therefore declared to be a true infanticide, one who had intentionally killed her child. The girl protested that she was not guilty. Several members of the court, who no longer believed in the efficacy of the tests, insisted that the girl must be convicted on another charge. And there were two other charges on either of which she could be sentenced to death, if found guilty. One was clandestine pregnancy, the other clandestine child-birth. The law against infanticide primarily sought the elimination of unmarried motherhood, for infanticide was only a result of the latter.

Accordingly the girl was asked if she had not heard the reading of the edict against the concealment of pregnancy.[39] She replied that she had not. Upon investigation it was discovered that the decree had not been read in her locality because the health of the town-crier, especially the weakness

[37] The digest was published under the title: "Nachtrag zu der Sammlung verschiedener gerichtlichen vollständigen Acten." Göttingen und Ruprecht, 1782, 2d ed., 1790. J. P. Vollhusen in a letter to Bürger (May 23, 1783) also speaks very highly of the case. See Strodtmann, "Briefe von und an Bürger," II, 113.

[38] Cf. Schlözer's *Stats-Anzeigen*, III, 155ff.; *idem*, 513ff.; V, 386ff.

[39] An edict was issued by Frederick William I, the predecessor of Frederick the Great, in 1720, in which it was required that the edict be read four times each year from every pulpit in the kingdom. Cf. *infra*, p. 33. A similar decree was issued by Louis XIV in France, 1708. See Froitzheim, "Goethe und Heinrich Leopold Wagner," p. 43.

of his voice, hindered him from performing this important duty. The judges decided that this made no difference, ignorance of the law excused no man. They overruled all objections and sentenced the girl to death on the charge of clandestine child-birth. Several days later she was executed by decapitation "as her well-deserved punishment and for the sake of others as a frightening example." The reporter for Schlözer's *Stats-Anzeigen* entitled his report "Justiz-Mord." In Amberg, where the trial and execution took place, there was a great revolt. Men who were prominently connected with the trial were exiled. Throughout Germany the case caused much discussion, for it was typical of the injustice inflicted on infanticides.

In the following pages I shall try to supply in detail the historical setting which is necessary to a perfect understanding of Goethe's pathetic tragedy of Gretchen. To what state of public opinion on the subject of child-murder did he address himself? If that opinion was hard and cruel as compared with that of our own time, to what is the fact due? What were its antecedents in social and religious usage, in legislation and in the administration of the law? When did the revolt against the inhuman treatment of unmarried mothers set in, what form did it take, who were its leaders, and what its effects? Finally, I shall discuss more fully than has been done hitherto the poems, plays and novels which deal with the subject and reflect the changing phases of public opinion with regard to it. In this way I seek to make a contribution to the history of modern humanitarianism in one of its most interesting and important aspects.

CHAPTER I

TRADITIONAL STATUS OF THE UNMARRIED MOTHER

Whether mothers were married or unmarried in the first stage of the evolution of the human race is a question that has been debated much during the last two centuries. Our final decision, if it ever can be final, will depend much on our definition of marriage. If we accept Westermarck's definition that marriage "is a more or less durable connection between male and female lasting beyond the mere act of propagation till after the birth of the offspring,"[1] and if it is true that this connection was an institution of nature, then the first human mother was married. But Todd[2] and with him most modern students of anthropology deny that marriage was an institution of nature and assert that "some form of sex-pairing and the maternal relation existed long before the marriage institution was consummated." According to these scholars the most primitive family consisted of a mother and her child, the father having been merely an instinctive progenitor, who knew nothing about his duties as the "head of the house." There are a number of good reasons for this attitude. The first is the disproof of the popular belief that natural attraction exerted an influence not only in bringing about sex union but in keeping the male and female together for the purpose of assuring the birth and growth of the child. The fact is that woman is repugnant to the natural man during pregnancy and the duty of the husband to his wife during that period and of the father to help care for the child was imposed by society and not by nature.

A second reason is given by Hartland,[3] who has recently

[1] Edward Westermarck, "The History of Human Marriage." London, 1891, 2d ed., 1894, p. 19.

[2] Arthur James Todd, "The Primitive Family as an Educational Agency." New York and London, 1913, p. 21.

[3] Edwin Sidney Hartland, "Primitive Paternity. The Myth of Supernatural Birth in relation to the History of the Family." London, 1910.

collected a wealth of material on the subject of primitive paternity, all of which goes to prove that all primitive peoples believed that impregnation was the result of some supernatural agency, they being ignorant of the fact that it resulted from sex union.

These and other reasons have led scholars to conclude that marriage or the union of father and mother jointly to bear the burdens of family life was brought about "by a more or less unconscious attempt to solve that group of life problems connected with self-maintenance and the perpetuation of the species." It was the law of necessity which forced the father to become an integral part of the human family. Marriage in that case must have been a social and not a natural institution and the first human mother was unmarried. The performance of a fixed ceremony to legalize marriage is a much later development and was admittedly an institution of society.

From these statements two important facts may be deduced. First, the institution of the family was based on the protection and care of the child, the mother instinctively performing these functions. Second, the most primitive father became a bona fide member of the family by protecting her who was soon to be a mother by him, and assisting in the protection and care of their joint offspring. As far back as we are able to trace the history of man the father who left the mother of his child in the lurch was considered a monster. We may believe in anonymous paternity among our earliest ancestors and still be compelled to admit that long before the beginning of our era our forebears had learned by experience that a family which consisted of a father, a mother and their child was a more perfect institution to guarantee the perpetuation of the race than a family which consisted of a mother and her babe, with the father roaming the wilderness.

Since the family is based on protection, a father or husband, if he was able, could care for several or many women as well as for one. Darwin believed that "men aboriginally lived in small communities, each with a single wife, or if powerful, with several, whom he jealously guarded against all other men."[4] He made the protection dependent upon jealousy

4 Cf. Descent of Man, II, 346.

instead of necessity. In either case a man had as many wives as he could protect. And men really had more than one wife among primitive peoples. But they were not necessarily of the same rank. It was only natural that the primitive man should differentiate among his wives. The distinction between legal and illegal or natural wives came into existence in this way, and it was based on the fact that the legal wife inherited the property of her husband while the other wives did not. In order to make a wife legal it was necessary to comply with a fixed ceremony, to enter into a contract, just as we make a contract before we can enjoy property rights. Legal marriage was based on property rights. This explains the universal custom among primitive men of having legal (right) and natural wives (concubines). A woman became a man's natural wife by sex union and his subsequent protection of her. She might never become his legal wife, but she was nevertheless his wife. The children of both wives, the legal and the natural, at first enjoyed the same privileges; they both inherited from the father, although the eldest son usually succeeded the father in his estate. This was especially true among the Hebrews.[5] In the earliest records of the ancient Teutons we already read of legal and natural children, the former being called so because of their legal mother, the latter after their natural mother. The legal mother was entitled to dower, the legal children to the inheritance of property. In all other respects the natural mother enjoyed the same privileges with the legal mother, the natural children with the legal children, foremost of which privileges was the father's protection. There is nothing in the history of our ancient Teutonic fathers that would lead us to believe that they did not protect and care for their wives and children.[6]

[5] Cf. Genesis 21, 10. Abraham had two sons, Isaac by his legal wife, Sarah, and Ishmael by Sarah's handmaid, Hagar. Their equality of rights is indicated by Sarah's request to Abraham: "Cast out the handmaid and her son, for the son of the handmaid shall not be heir with my son, even with Isaac." Cf. also Gen. 29 and 30. Jacob had two legal wives, Leah and Rachel, and two natural wives, Zilpah and Bilhah. By these four wives he had twelve children, all enjoying the same privileges. He was father, and therefore protector, to them all.

[6] Cf. Joseph Freisen, "Geschichte des Canonischen Eherechts bis zum Verfall der Glossenlitteratur." Tübingen, 1888, for a detailed discussion of this phase of the sex problem among primitive peoples, especially p. 110.

When primitive peoples discovered that pregnancy was due to sex union, they set up the rule that, since the father and mother had joined themselves together to protect and care for the child as well as for sex union, the sole object of marriage was the propagation and rearing of children. That marriage would automatically cease to exist when all the children were grown up and no more children could be propagated did not occur to them. Their erroneous conclusion was based on an erroneous observation. They saw that the propagation and rearing of children did consume all the time of married people, but failed to realize that it did not need to do so.

Such notions were the most current until the institution of the Christian church. Christ did not marry, but no word of his can be construed as hostile to marriage. What he says of sexual transgressions, notably his refusal to condemn the woman taken in adultery, evinces a tolerant spirit. Of the unmarried mother he never spoke at all. Christ condemned the manner of thinking which made sexual sins possible, he did not condemn those who had committed these sins.

It was quite impossible for the church to fix its attitude toward the sex problem, especially toward marriage, by the scant statements of Christ. It was the teaching of Paul rather than that of Christ which formed the basis of canon law on sex matters. Paul taught that marriage was good, but celibacy better. "It is good for a man not to touch a woman"; he wrote, "nevertheless to avoid fornication, let each man have his own wife and let each woman have her own husband. He that giveth his virgin in marriage doeth well, but he that giveth her not in marriage doeth better. . . . If they (the unmarried and widows) cannot contain, let them marry; for it is better to marry than to burn."[7] Augustine accepted Paul's teaching and added that "unmarried children would shine in heaven as beaming stars, whilst their parents would look like the dim ones." Ambrosius set up the rule: nuptiæ terram replent, virginitas paradisum.[8] So certain were these old church fathers that "marriage was profane and impure"

[7] I Corinthians, VII.
[8] Cf. Freisen, *loc. cit.*, p. 25.

that Tertullian insisted that, in order to keep morality on earth, celibacy must be chosen even if mankind should perish.[9]

There are good reasons why some people should not marry, that is, should refrain from the gratification of a natural and necessary instinct and renounce the ethical benefits accruing from such a union. We honor the man or woman who refrains from marriage because of some physical or mental ailment which is inheritable and would cause suffering to progeny. We also admire the man or woman who voluntarily refrains from marriage for the sake of some nobly conceived life-work which is, or is sincerely believed to be, incompatible with marriage and the rearing of children. Such sacrifice is ethical and may be heroic.

Paul and the church fathers, however, did not place the main emphasis on this idea of sacrifice or renunciation for exceptional cases, they made it a fixed rule for everybody. They thought marriage was at best a make-shift, a state wherein it was permissible to satisfy impure and unholy desires, the satisfaction of which a carnal nature had made necessary. They were not at all concerned about the future of the race, they sincerely believed that the world would come to an end even in their day and generation. They failed to see that the sex impulse is holy, if anything is holy, since without it no holiness, or religion or philosophy would exist. Instead of making marriage a sacred institution in which the powers of man normally reach their greatest development, they made it a concession to his weakness. Paul said: "He that is unmarried careth for the things that belong to the Lord, how he may please the Lord: but he that is married careth for the things that are of the world, how he may please his wife." The experience of the race has proved that Paul and the church fathers were mistaken. Celibacy, except as a necessity or a sacrifice, is neither a natural nor a reasonable institution. On the contrary, the chief factor which increases "immorality is the growing number of unmarried people. It is proved that in the cities of Europe, [and our cities are no exception] prostitution increases according as the number of marriages

[9] Westermarck, *loc. cit.*, p. 154.

decreases. It has also been established, . . . that the fewer the marriages contracted in a year, the greater is the ratio of illegitimate births. Thus, by making celibacy more common, civilization promotes sexual irregularity."[10]

The early church fathers made another mistake. They asserted that only such marriage as the church sanctioned was legal, all other marriage being fornication. Therefore this rule was laid down: Marriage in order to have the approval of the church must be legal, that is, a man and a woman must go through a fixed ceremony, so that both have property rights as to each other. The church dictated what this ceremony should be and therefore secured absolute authority in sex matters. The institution of marriage as a sacrament was a much later development.[11] The main element in this sacrament was the teaching of the indissolubility of marriage. While heretofore property rights of the wife as to her husband depended upon the legality of marriage, the legality of marriage now became dependent upon a ceremony, arbitrarily dictated by the church.

By this teaching the church immediately came into conflict with the practice of concubinage, which existed among all the peoples over which it exerted its influence. Since concubines, that is, natural wives, among the Romans enjoyed the same privileges as legal wives, except the right of inheriting property, the church asserted that such concubinage was negation of marriage. Concubinage was such a fixed practice that the church was compelled to permit it even after it decided in favor of legal marriage. But the hierarchy constantly worked against it, generally by preventing those who administered for the church from advancing in position if they practiced concubinage. It took five hundred years to eliminate the practice among the priesthood and to make celibacy obligatory; and even after this many priests must have practiced it, for it is a matter of common knowledge that practically every council of the church immediately preceding the Reformation considered the matter of permitting priests

[10] Westermarck, *loc. cit.*, p. 70.
[11] Cf. Freisen, *loc. cit.*, p. 29ff.

to marry because of the existence of so much immorality. By this constant opposition to concubinage, the church contributed much to the establishment of monogamy as the standard marriage. The assertion that the Reformation abolished concubinage in Europe is untenable, for concubinage or some modification of it has not ceased to exist in European countries to this day. The mistresses of the eighteenth and the paramours of the nineteenth and twentieth centuries were and are concubines or natural wives under a different name.

The mistake of the church fathers lies not so much in placing emphasis on the marriage ceremony as a necessary condition of legality, but rather in the grounding of this ceremony on the traditions of the Old Testament, in preference to a first-hand knowledge of contemporary human life. Instead of encouraging its constituents to marry in accordance with the best known requirements of a successful marriage, the church virtually dictated who could and who could not marry by preventing from marriage all those who came in conflict with the superstitions of a primitive people who belonged to a very different civilization.

Another problem which confronted the church was the practice of exposure and killing of children by legal parents. Sumner asserts that "Abortion, exposure and infanticide were and still are so nearly universal in savage life, either as egoistic or group policy, that exceptions to the practice of these vices are noteworthy phenomena."[13]

[13] William Graham Sumner, "Folkways." Boston, 1907, p. 315. Cf. also Joseph Müller, "Das sexuelle Leben der christlichen Kulturvölker," Leipzig, 1904, page 110. We read: "Noch zu erwähnen ist das Recht der Kinderaussetzung, das bei den alten Germanen, wie bei allen Naturvölkern in Übung stand."; Paul Wilutzky, "Vorgeschichte des Rechts." Breslau, 1903, II, 5f.: "One can calmly assert, . . . terrible as it may seem now . . . that infanticide, particularly that of girls, was a legal arrangement of convenience among all primitive peoples of the world." John Ferguson McLennan, "Studies in Ancient History," London, 1896, Chapter VII, entitled Female Infanticide. See further Edward Westermarck, "The History of Human Marriage," London, 1894, p. 311ff.; Arthur James Todd, "The Primitive Family as an Educational Agency," New York and London, 1913, p. 126f.; Elsie Clews Parsons, "The Family," New York and London, 1906, p. 44f.; Albert Hermann Post, "Grundriss der ethnologischen Jurisprudenz," Oldenburg und Leipzig, 1895, p. 8ff.; C. N. Starcke, "The Primitive Family," New York, 1889, p. 129ff.; etc.

This fact, I fear, is not known sufficiently well among civilized nations today. If it were some of the peculiar notions and prejudices on the sex problem could not exist.[14]

Exposure and infanticide were at first due to natural causes. Foremost among these was malformation. It was the suffering which the imperfectibility of the child entailed upon both itself and its fellows that caused its elimination from the human family. According to the twelve tablets of Romulus infanticide and exposure were very common practices in the early days of Rome. The father was permitted under certain conditions to put to death children over three years of age and to expose and kill children under three years if they had been declared monstrous by five neighbors. "Seneca refers to the killing of defective children as a wise and unquestioned custom."[15] Aristotle had long before expressed a similar opinion. "A missionary recently returned from New Guinea reported a case where the parents of a sickly, peevish child, probably teething, calmly decided to kill it."[16]

The second natural cause of these practices was overpopulation, which had poverty as its counterpart. Parents exposed or killed their children if they were too poor to support them, or if they anticipated poverty, or if they felt that the burdens incurred by caring for more than a few children were too great. "Australian life formerly was full of privations on account of limited supplies of food and water. Therefore a woman could not carry two children. If she had one who could not yet march and bore another, the latter was killed. In Dutch New Guinea the women will not rear more than two or three children each. . . . They shirk the trouble of rearing them. Wilkins says that six-sevenths of the population of

---

[14] Probably Tacitus led historians of German primitive life astray by his assertion that the old Teutons did not restrict the number of children or commit infanticide. Modern scholars have tried to correct this erroneous opinion. Cf. Karl Weinhold, "Deutsche Frauen im Mittelalter," I, 91; Jakob Grimm, "Deutsche Rechtsalterthümer," Leipzig, 1899, II, 254f.; Konrad Maurer, "Die Wasserweihe des germanischen Heidenthumes," München, 1880, p. 4; G. Steinhausen, "Germanische Kultur in der Urzeit," Leipzig, 1910, p. 59f. in No. 75 of "Aus Natur und Geisteswelt."

[15] Cf. Sumner, *loc. cit.*, p. 319.

[16] *Idem*, p. 317.

India have for ages practiced female infanticide. German rulers formerly exposed infants lest dependent persons should be multiplied."[17]

A third natural cause was superstition. Twins were always looked upon with awe. Some of the ancients argued: So many children, so many fathers.[18] Therefore one or both children were killed. Dreams when unfavorable were taken as bad omens and the child was killed.[19] These examples could be multiplied indefinitely.

People naively looked upon the child as the fruit and property of parents, and found in abortion, exposure and infanticide nothing sinful. The moral duty to the new-born child was a development of a later civilization. The moral duty to the unborn is becoming a vital part of our civilization today for the first time in the history of the race. It is to these horrible practices, even if natural, that Tyler applied the dictum: Infanticide arises from hardness of life rather than from hardness of heart.[20]

But these practices did not remain within the naturally prescribed boundaries. With the refinement of society they fell into abuse. Where before only the father had the right to commit these practices as part of his *patria potestas*, it was now acquired by the grandmother of the child, and then by the brother of the mother of the child.[21] Infanticide now ceased to be a rightful privilege, it became a privileged right, by which a child might be eliminated from society to the end of procuring any selfish desire. Just preceding the introduction of Christianity in Greece and Italy, "children were exposed and killed on account of luxury, egoism and vice." Pagan and Christian authorities speak of infanticide as the crying vice of the empires.[22] Among the Scandinavians the

[17] Cf. Sumner, *loc. cit.*, p. 315f.

[18] Cf. Alwin Schultz, "Das höfische Leben." Leipzig, 1889, I, 145.

[19] Karl Weinhold, "Deutsche Frauen im Mittelalter," I, 93f. Cf. Schiller, "Die Braut von Messina."

[20] Cf. Todd, *loc. cit.*, p. 128.

[21] Liafburh, the mother of Liudger, narrowly escaped death by drowning because the grandmother was fearful that she would have all granddaughters and no grandsons. Cf. Vita S. Liutgeri in Pertz' "Monumenta Germaniae Historica," II, 406, cap. 6 and 7.

[22] Cf. Sumner, p. 319.

father would expose a child to take revenge for an insult on the part of his wife.[23] Or the child of a concubine might be killed because of the jealousy of the right wife.[24] A brother habitually killed the child of his sister if its birth caused the death of the mother.[25] The old Vikings extended a spear to the new-born boy. If the child seized it, it was allowed to live. Because Ölver, a powerful Viking, did not administer this test, he was nicknamed "barnakarl," children's man.[26] More commonly the life of the child was made dependent upon the performance of a fixed ceremony similar to our modern ceremony of baptism. This ceremony is usually called "Wasserweihe."[27]

Immediately after the birth of a child the father was summoned, and the child was placed either on his knee or on the floor before him. If he decided that the child should live he took it up in his arms. Then water was poured on the child, a name was given and generally it was presented with a gift. Not until then was nourishment given to the child. If the child was not taken up by the father, it was immediately exposed or killed without baptism and without food. If either of these two conditions had been fulfilled it became illegal to kill a child. Another important element was attached to this ceremony. From the time that a child was baptized, it had property rights. The importance attached to this fact is attested by the long survival of the custom of reckoning the attainment of property rights from the time of baptism. In Sweden this custom remained until 1734, in Norway until 1854, and in Denmark until 1857.

So firmly were these practices fixed in the *mores* that the church was unable to convince its constituents of the wrongness of them until it introduced a mystic religious element. In the year 418 A. D. Augustine succeeded at the great Carthaginian general synod in securing the adoption of a canon

[23] Cf. Finnboga s. hins ramma 2/4.

[24] Cf. Vatnsdaela 37/59.

[25] Cf. Holmverja 8/19.

[26] Cf. Karl Weinhold, "Altnordisches Leben." Berlin, 1856, p. 260.

[27] Cf. Konrad Maurer, "Ueber die Wasserweihe des germanischen Heidenthumes." München, 1880.

which asserted that children who died unbaptizedwent to a middle place, half way between the place of punishment and the place of bliss. The old Teutons under the influence of Christianity believed that unbaptized children went to a place between Gohoater and Gahül, the clouds and heaven.[28] There was introduced a custom of refusing to bury unbaptized children in sacred ground. But just as natural sympathy held back the old church fathers from condemning the unbaptized child directly to hell, so this custom did not force the burial of these children in non-sacred ground. They were placed in the cemetery wall, half way between sacred and non-sacred ground. Laistner tells of a place in Tirol at Reit where not so long ago there could be found alongside the large cemetery a small plot of ground, which was called "the church-yard of the innocents," because in it only infants who died unbaptized were buried. Such burying places were also to be found in many other villages. Maurer asserts that the proposition that unbaptized children must not be buried in the conse- crated cemeteries was so firmly established that there was even doubt as to whether an unborn child should be buried with its dead mother in the same cemetery.[29]

This unbiblical and unchristian teaching of the church that children who died unbaptized went to a place somewhere between heaven and hell "affected the minds of the masses more than the suffering or death of the infants ever had." The intensity of its influence is attested by the fact that this teaching is still believed by members in many divisions of the Christian church. Infanticide by legal parents has practically ceased in civilized countries, but abortion, its substitute, has not. It must be admitted that the church contributed much to end this practice but its influence did not do it alone. Sumner thinks that "in reality nothing has put an end to infanticide but the advance in the arts (increased economic power), by virtue of which parents can provide for children."[30]

[28] Cf. Ludwig Laistner in an article "Nobishaus und Verwandtes." *Germania*, XXVI, 85ff.

[29] Maurer, *loc. cit.*, p. 23f.: "And if a woman with child dies, she shall be buried as other people, and the child shall not be taken from her."

[30] "Folkways," p. 321.

We have considered the sex problem from the angle of legitimacy, in order to bring into relief the development of the institution of marriage, and the origin of the terms "legal," "natural," "illegal," "married" and "unmarried," as applied to the mother. As far back as there are records of men any sex union which did not result in marriage, if pregnancy resulted, was looked upon with animosity and met with severe punishment. Sex union which involved adultery was probably the first transgression to which the term illegitimacy was applied. Fornication of the unmarried came later under the legal taboo. The old Hebrews looked upon illegitimate impregnation, that is rape and adultery, as the greatest of crimes and punished it with stoning to death or burning alive.[31] Among other primitive peoples the man who committed adultery or fornication was killed or flogged, his head was shaved or his ears were cut off, one of his eyes was put out, his legs were speared, etc. A woman who was found guilty of either of these crimes was beaten or killed, disfigured by cutting off her nose or her ears, her head was shaved, etc.[32] Tacitus says that "the punishment for adultery among the Teutons is immediate and is usually left to the men. After shearing off her hair and undressing her, the husband kicks his wife out of the house in the presence of all the neighbors and drives her with heavy blows through the whole village."[33] Among the West Goths the adulteress was treated very harshly. Her shawl was torn from her shoulders and the back part of her shirt was cut off.[34] The oldest Teutonic law required that a man who had impregnated a maiden should be killed like an adulterer. The fallen girl was either killed or exiled from home and country by being sold into slavery.[35]

The principle upon which these punishments were based was that every offense must be punished according to its gravity. Fundamentally it was a law of revenge, an eye for

---

[31] For the attitude of the Hebrews toward adultery see Gen. 34; 38; Judges 19, 22f.; Judith 13, 1f.; Numbers 25.

[32] Cf. Westermarck, pp. 121, 122.

[33] Germania, chapter 19.

[34] See Weinhold, "Altnordisches Leben," p. 250.

[35] *Idem*, p. 255.

an eye and a tooth for a tooth. No attempt was made to examine into the justification of an offense.

With the coming of Christ this old law was contradicted. He gave a new rule, which was quite the opposite of the old law, by declaring that no sinner had any right to pass judgment on another. He insisted that sin did not begin in the hand, which committed the visible act, but in the heart. He placed the emphasis not on the justice of revenge but on the improvement and reclamation of the criminal. This is the root of our modern "Besserungstheorie," or theory of betterment. The old Hebrew theory of punishment was based on natural impulse, the theory advanced by Christ on reason. The evidence goes to show that the early church honestly attempted to apply Christ's theory of punishment until the number of unmarried mothers, because of the encouragement of celibacy, became so numerous that something had to be done. The church started out to make of marriage an institution quite contrary to nature, and naturally lost its fight to eliminate the unmarried mother from the sex problem. The law givers of the church instituted a new theory of punishment, the "Abschreckungstheorie." This theory involved the principle that the larger the number of criminals of a certain kind the more severe the punishment should be. The severity of punishment was not graded according to the gravity of the crime, but according to its frequency. No attempt was made to examine into its justification. This theory was a greater injustice to criminals than the theory of revenge, for in its application there was room for the most outrageous arbitrariness.

Because of all crimes her crime could be most easily detected, the unmarried mother suffered most under this new theory of punishment. Man could very easily conform to the rules of the church, first because his sexual transgression could not be detected, and then because he could resort to perjury to evade the law. But the woman could not do this. In due time her relation would be revealed to the whole world, there would be a living witness to rise up against her in the day of judgment. Because the woman usually revealed that there had been sex union, while the man could not be found out, all primitive peoples asserted that woman and not man was the transgressor and one of the foremost civilized nations of Europe until very recently acted on the Napoleonic edict: "la recherche de la paternité est interdite." All religious teachers of old agreed with Augustine that woman was the "gate of the devil." The church sincerely believed that it had finally located the root of the whole sex problem; it was the unmarried mother. The whole punishment of sex union fell on her. If the man could be found out, he too would suffer, but his crime was not at all comparable to hers. But the greatest injustice was inflicted on the illegitimate children. At the synod held in England 787–788, for instance, the right of inheritance of property was withdrawn from illegitimate children.[36] This was followed shortly by a refusal of state and church to accept them into citizenship or communion.

Then the large number of unmarried mothers, which steadily increased as the church victoriously marched forward in its establishment of celibacy, tried to conform to the requirement of the church by concealing pregnancy, and child-birth, and then by killing their children secretly. This was the beginning of illegitimate infanticide. While the church was trying to stamp out concubinage and legal infanticide, it made possible a terrifying number of unmarried mothers, forced them to conceal their condition and to kill their illegitimate offspring, and then began to punish them more severely than any other criminal. I know of no more terrible page in history than the attempt of the church through canon and civil law to define marriage and to stamp out a delict which it made possible by this definition. Our modern problem of illegitimacy goes back to this very great mistake of our venerated church fathers, and the sooner we members of that same church to which they belonged admit their mistake and actively attempt to correct it, the sooner shall we bring back that church to a place where it will truly deserve the name of Christ. The activity of the modern church in this direction redounds to its credit.

[36] Freisen, *loc. cit.*, p. 687.

The usual punishments for infanticide during the Middle Ages and even into the eighteenth century were: sacking (Säcken), an infanticide being sewed up in a sack and thrown into the water; burying alive (Lebendigbegraben); empaling (Pfählen), a pointed stick being driven through the heart; and burning alive (Feuertod).[37]

Scherr asserts that "in Frankfurt on the Main the first case of infanticide reported to the authorities was in 1444. The decree of the courts was that the girl should suffer death by drowning, but because of the ardent intercession of the women of the city she was pardoned. In Nürnberg during the fifteenth century not one case was reported to the authorities, in the sixteenth, six, in the seventeenth, thirty-six."[38] Pescheck reported that in Lusatia the usual punishment was sacking or burying alive if the girl had murdered her child, and humiliating public church penance if she had not. "In Zittau," he writes, "there was not far from the gallows a so-called sacking pond (Säcklache). The infanticide was stuffed into a black sack together with a dog, a cat, a rooster or a viper. The sack had to remain under water for six hours and the choir boys sang: Aus tiefer Noth schrei ich zu Dir. Then the deceased was interred. Burying alive of infanticides occurred frequently in Zittau in the sixteenth century. . . . A number of times a pale was also driven through the heart of the girl after she had been buried alive."[39] Other examples are to be found in the archives of Zürich. Here it is told how infanticides were bound hand and foot and thrown into the Limmat near a fisherman's hut, which with its encircling hedge stood on an island in the middle of the stream. This custom endured until 1785. In 1511 this punishment was inflicted on a girl who for the third time had corseted so tightly that it was impossible for her illegitimate child to be born alive. In 1424 an infanticide was buried alive with a bed of thorns over and under her. The hands of another girl, who in her despair

---

[37] See Julius Wehrli, "Der Kindsmord; dogmatisch-kritische Studie." Frauenfeld, 1889, p. 15.

[38] Johannes Scherr, "Deutsche Kultur- und Sittengeschichte." Leipzig, 1873, p. 194.

[39] Cf. *Anzeiger für Kunde der deutschen Vorzeit*, 1854, p. 114.

buried her babe alive, were bound together, and slipped over her knees, then a pale was thrust between the arms and thighs, and she was thrown into the water and held there until death came.[40]   Many unmarried mothers after succeeding in their concealment of pregnancy and child-birth felt the maternal instinct too strongly to kill the fruit of their forbidden love. Instead they placed their children before the doors of the city council houses.   Weinhold reports that "in Basel such exposure of children reached such proportions at the beginning of the fifteenth century that a decree of the city council threatened that every woman who in the future should thus expose her child, if it were found out, would be thrown into the Rhine."[41]

Simple decapitation was considered a merciful punishment. In an archive of Bischofszell, canton Thurgau, it is stated that an infanticide had been condemned to die on a "bed of thorns."   The upper bailiff however in the name of the bishop tempered the punishment and substituted simple decapitation.[42]   These examples could be multiplied indefinitely.   In the archives of all the imperial cities of Europe there is recorded the story of these hapless unmarried mothers.[43]

These cruel forms of punishment by the civil courts, and it is well to remember that these courts were dominated absolutely by the church, were paralleled by the most humiliating public church penance for the unmarried mother who did not kill her child.   Laukhard in true Storm and Stress fashion gives us a vivid picture of this punishment which so often drove girls to infanticide.   "Those who had made an unprivileged, *i. e.*, an illegitimate, contribution to the increase

---

[40] These cases were reported by von Meyer von Knonau in the *Anzeiger für Kunde der deutschen Vorzeit*, 1855, p. 175.

[41] See Karl Weinhold, "Deutsche Frauen im Mittelalter." Wien, 1882, I, p. 95.

[42] See Wehrli, "Der Kindsmord; etc.," p. 139.

[43] See for instance *Zeitschrift für deutsche Kulturgeschichte*, Nürnberg, 1859, IV, p. 774f.: "Zur Kriminalstatistik der beiden Städte Zeiz und Naumburg während der Jahre 1549–1664."   Here is a record of four cases of infanticide in Zeiz, three of the girls were drowned, the fourth died before the execution and was therefore buried under the gallows.   In Naumburg there were three cases during this time.   One was decapitated, another was drowned, the third was whipped only, because she had notified the authorities of her condition.

of the population were compelled to submit to public church penance in the presence of the whole congregation. During this outrageous exhibition (hildebrandischer Unfug) songs of penance were sung in hurdy-gurdy fashion, then a typically narrow sermon was thundered forth on this vice of fornication, which had been arbitrarily called so. In the sermon all the passages of the Old Testament in which this awful sin was disgustingly depicted were recited with clock-like regularity and accompanied by a drastic monkish exegesis. Then the penitent had to confess before the whole congregation—that which everyone already knew—that she was a harlot and he a fornicator; thereafter she was absolved from her sinful guilt and permitted to partake of the sacrament of the Lord's Supper. . . . Experience has proved that just this church penance gave occasion for secret sins, attempts at abortion, infanticide, public contempt and poor education of natural or illegitimate children, emigration, yes, at times for suicide or dangerous illness, which resulted from melancholy and anxiety."[44]

From a written petition to Duke Karl August drawn up by Goethe we learn that the unmarried mother who was automatically excommunicated from the church, could again become a member by undergoing the excruciating church penance. Undoubtedly many a poor girl yielded to this requirement because she believed, as she had been taught, that only those who were in the fold of the church could reach heaven, while many another attempted to remain chaste in the eyes of the church by concealing her condition and then killing her child.

From all that we have said on the punishment of the unmarried mother it is easy to see that it was not uniform in the Middle Ages and the succeeding centuries. This was so because there was no uniform criminal law in Germany nor in Europe at this time. Crimes were punished differently by each city or town, the only element of uniformity being the application of the same theory of punishment, the "Ab-

---

[44] "Der Wild und Rheingraf Carl Magnus vom Magister Laukhard." Herausgegeben von Viktor Petersen, Stuttgart, 1911, p. 62ff.

schreckungstheorie." With a view to establishing uniformity Emperor Charles V and his advisors in 1532 published a code of criminal law known as "die peinliche Gerichtsordnung Karls V" (P. G. O.), the Constitutio Criminalis Carolina (C.C.C.), or in short the Carolina. This code met with the approval of the imperial estates at the diet of Regensburg in 1532. Articles 35, 36 and 131 are concerned with the discovery and punishment of infanticide. The first two articles made it possible to convict at will practically every unmarried woman of infanticide provided there was a sufficient number of people who were willing to perjure themselves, for the law was very willing to convict and execute. Article 131 decrees that infanticides are regularly to be buried alive or empaled. In order to prevent desperation, however, they shall be drowned if it is possible to get to a stream or river, in which case they shall be torn with glowing tongs beforehand. Wherever the delict happens often the authorities shall regularly decree burying alive or empalement.[45]

[45] Since the revolt against antiquated laws in the period of Storm and Stress goes back to this code, it seems advisable to give the articles pertaining to infanticide in full. Art. 35: Item so man eyn dirn so für eyn jungfraw geht, imm argkwon hat, dass sie heymlich eyn kindt gehabt, vnnd ertödt habe, soll man sonderlich erkunden, ob sie mit einem grossen vngewonlichen leib gesehen worden sei, Mer, ob jr der leib kleyner worden, vnd darnach bleych vnnd schwach gewest sei. So solchs vnd dergleichen erfunden wirdet, wo dann die selbig dirnn eyn person ist, darzu man sich der verdachten thatt versehen mag, Soll sie durch verstendig frawen an heymlichen stetten, als zu weither erfarung dienstlich ist, besichtigt werden, würd sie dann daselbst auch argkwönig erfunden, vnnd will der thatt dannocht nit bekennen, mag man sie peinlich fragen. Art. 36: Item wo aber das kindtlein, so kürtzlich ertödt worden ist, dass der mutter die milch inn den prüsten noch nit vergangen, die mag an jren prüsten gemolcken werden, welcher dann inn den prüsten recht vollkommene milch funden wirdet, die hat desshalb eyn starck vermutung peinlicher frag halber wider sich. Nach dem aber etliche leibärtzt sagen, dass auss etlichen natürlichen vrsachen etwann eyne, die keyn kindt getragen, milch in prüsten haben möge, darumb so sich eyn dirnn inn disen fellen also entschuldigt, so soll desshalb durch die hebammen oder sunst weither erfarung geschehen. Art. 131: Item welches weib jre kind, das leben vnd glidmass empfangen hett, heymlicher bosshafftiger williger weiss ertödtet, die werden gewonlich lebendig begraben vnnd gepfelt, Aber darinnen verzweiffelung zuuerhütten, mögen dieselben übelthätterin inn welchem gericht die bequemlicheyt des wassers darzu vorhanden ist, ertrenckt werden, Wo aber solche übel offt geschehe, wollen wir die gemelten gewonheyt des vergrabens vnnd pfelens, vmb mer forcht willen, solcher bosshafftigen weiber auch zulassen, oder aber das vor dem erdrencken die

The most important characteristic of these decrees is a sentence in Art. 131 which made the concealment of pregnancy, child-birth and then infanticide equally punishable. To punish girls who had been forced to kill their children was bad enough, but to inflict the same severe punishment for the concealment of pregnancy gave judges who already were arbitrary enough an opportunity to enter on a veritable "reign of terror." Benedict Carpzov (1595–1666), who credited himself with having read the Bible fifty-three times, assisted in executing not less than twenty thousand women, most of them charged with witchcraft, a large number with infanticide. It was he who exceeded the decree of the Carolina by ordering that the infanticide should be drowned with three animals, a cat, a dog, a monkey or a viper, and that she should sew up her own sack of linen or leather. This manner of punishment was common in Saxony until 1734 and in Prussia until the time of Frederick the Great.[46] Pescheck asserted that it was inflicted for the last time in Zittau in 1749, but not officially abolished until 1761.

That Carpzov's influence was very great is best evidenced by a vehement philippic which may be found in Moritz August von Thümmel's "Die Reise in die mittäglichen Provinzen von Frankreich."[47] We read: "His (Carpzov's) criminal erudi-

übelthätterin mit glüenden zangen gerissen werde, alles nach radt der recht-uerstendigen. . . . Doch so eyn weibssbild eyn lebendig glitmessig kindtlein also heymlich tregt, auch mit willen alleyn, vnnd on hilff anderer weiber gebürt, welche on hilffliche geburt, mit tödtlicher verdechtlicheyt geschehen muss, So ist desshalb keyn glaublichere vrsach, dann dass die selbig mutter durch bosshafftigen fürsatz vermeynt, mit tödtung des vnschuldigen kindtleins daran sie vor inn oder nach der geburt schuldig wirt, jre geübte leichtvertigkeyt verborgen zuhalten. Darumb wann eyn solche mörderin auff gedachter jrer angemasten vnbeweisten frevenlichen entschuldigung bestehn bleiben wolt, so soll man sie auff obgemelte gnugsame antzeygung bestimpts vnchristlichen vnnd vnmenschlichen erfunden übels vnd mordts halber, mit peinlicher ernstlicher frag zu bekanntnuss der wahrheyt zwingen, Auch auff bekenntnuss des selben mordts zu entlicher todtstraff, als obsteht vrtheylen. Doch wo eyns solchen weibs schuld oder vnschuld halb gezweiffelt würd, so sollen die Richter vnd vrtheyler mit antzeygung aller vmbstende bei den rechtverstendigen oder sunst wie hernach gemelt wirdet, radts pflegen. The decrees are in Heinrich Zoepfl, "Die P. G. O. Kaiser Karl's V. usw." Heidelberg, 1842.

[46] Cf. Grimm, "Rechtsalterthümer," II, 279.

[47] See A. M. v. Thümmels sämmtliche Werke. Leipzig, 1839, II, 250ff.

tion super-abounded in thick volumes behind grated book-cases of our law room, and every weak head which came too near was benumbed by the poisonous exhalation from their pages. This Moloch of his time . . . even after his death exerted his baneful influence through his disciples, who in their blindness of spirit and in their intellectual conceit followed in his footsteps. The justices instead of thinking for themselves found it more convenient to refer to him who had already considered all this that they should have reconsidered. The digests were simply interlarded with his arbitrary sentences (Machtsprüche) and every attorney, every judge obediently bowed his head before this despot. It would have been necessary for me to be a Hercules to kill this many-headed monster with one blow."

As long as there were such men at the head of state and church it was no wonder that the cruel forms of punishment which had been in use before the Carolina was published should continue afterward. Spielmann corroborates the fact that drowning was still the most common form of punishment of infanticides in 1550.[48] There is also evidence that they continued to bury girls alive. In Dietmarschen, as late as the seventeenth century, fallen girls were placed under the ice to meet with a miserable death.[49] An old decree of these same people, which was confirmed by Frederick II, King of the Danes in 1567, read: "Whoever kills her own child shall be buried alive under the gallows."[50] A broadside of 1610 tells of an infanticide at Brittalen, in the land of the Lithuanians, who placed the blame for the death of her child on way-faring traders. Later she was led to the dead child and

> Man zeigte jhr das todte Kind—
> Bald auss jhr Nasen roht Blut rinnt.
> Ohn Pein bekandte eben
> Wie sie dieses, sechse darzu,
> Schandtlich hab bracht umbs Leben.

[48] In *Nassovia*, IX, 1908, p. 146. Cf. also Abegg in *Zeitschrift für deutsches Recht*, XVIII, 423.

[49] Weinhold, "Altnordisches Leben," p. 255.

[50] Johannes Paulli Kressius, "Commentatio succincta in constitutionem criminalem Caroli V, etc." Hannover, 1736, p. 419.

Also hat sie jhr Urtheil schwer
Aussgstanden selbs nach anderen begehr,
Lebendig ward vergraben
Ein Bund Dorn under sie ist gelegt
Ein Rohr ins Maul gegeben.[51]

The most terrible of punishments, empalement, the inflic-
tion of which is referred to in the last line above, was practically forbidden by the Carolina. Another example to prove
that this prohibition was not effective is that of an infanticide
in Zittau, who was executed in 1573. Because empalement
was resorted to, the authorities abolished the supreme court,
which was later reinstated, however, by the payment of a sum
of money.[52] Grimm tells of another city which in 1554
decreed that those "who have had children and have killed
them, shall be placed alive in a pit, a pile of thorns shall be
placed on the body, both shall be covered with earth, and an
oaken pale shall be driven through the heart."[53] As late as
1714 a decree of empalement was sent to Prague.

In the early part of the seventeenth century simple decapitation became the normal punishment, although it was
usually accompanied by "tearing with glowing tongs." Such
punishment was looked upon as merciful.

In looking through the archives one seldom finds a case
where the seducer is mentioned. When he was found out
he was punished severely.[54] The reason he was so seldom
punished is to be found in the fact that the courts always
accepted the man's denial in preference to the woman's accu-
sation. It was a war against the unmarried mother and not
against the unmarried father.

The application of the "Abschreckungstheorie" was a com-
plete failure. At the beginning of the eighteenth century
J. S. F. Böhmer (1704–1772) asserted that infanticide was
mentioned because it was the most common of crimes. Still

[51] This is usually referred to as "das Motif von der Litthauischen Kindesmörderin." See *Alemannia*, Bonn, 1890, XVIII, 52. Cf. comments by J.
Elias in *Jahresberichte für neuere deutsche Litteraturgeschichte*, I, III, 31.

[52] See *Anzeiger für Kunde der deutschen Vorzeit*, 1854, 114.

[53] See Grimm, "Rechtsalterthümer," II, 271.

[54] *Idem*, II, 269, 271, 275.

better evidence is an edict by Frederick William I, King of
Prussia, the predecessor of Frederick the Great. The edict
was issued August 30, 1720, almost two hundred years after
the publication of the Carolina. It was entitled: "General
Edict against infanticide, in which the punishment of sacking
is ordered."[55] The first paragraph refers to the current custom of decreeing simple decapitation instead of sacking.
The second paragraph reads in part: "Since, we are sorry to
say, experience proves that this crime is becoming all too
common, and many children born out of marriage are killed
at birth by their wicked mothers, and since the blood of these
children cries for revenge, we should attempt to frighten these
dissolute minds." In a later paragraph the king decrees that
all girls who have given birth to an illegitimate child shall,
according to the circumstances, be scourged and then exiled
from home and country, even if no murder has taken place.
For the unmarried mothers, however, who had killed their
children, he decreed that on conviction the punishment of
sacking should invariably be ordered, leaving it to the reviewing tribunal to determine if leniency should be exercised,
"which we, because of the frequency of this horrible evil, are
not minded to do." The edict was to be published in the
usual manner, to be posted in all public places and read in all
the churches of the kingdom on each first day of penance.

Three years later, November 22, 1723, there was published
a "renovirtes und geschärftes" edict. The king complains
that the former edict did not produce the results which he
expected and "this vice so contrary to nature and in every way
so horrible still continues to increase." He urges the authorities to increase their zeal in trying to find out girls who are
about to become unmarried mothers, for "concealment of
pregnancy is a certain sign of intentional murder and only by
finding it out can this crime be prevented."

The popular attitude toward the unmarried mother and the
causes which led her to kill her child had not greatly changed
from the Middle Ages to the beginning of the eighteenth

[55] The decrees of King Frederick William I. are available in Mylius, "Corpus
Constitutionum Marchicarum, etc."

century. If Frederick William I had been a student of history he would have known that it was the Thirty Years' War, especially the presence of the thousands of unmarried soldiers, which had so greatly increased the number of unmarried mothers and of infanticides. There developed at the beginning of the eighteenth century a movement which had as its goal the discovery of the causes of infanticide as well as of crime in general. The jurist Leyser for the first time distinguished two kinds of infanticide: first, that committed by girls who had been innocently seduced; second, that committed by girls who practiced prostitution. He also suggested that the first class be punished by simple decapitation, because "most girls who commit the crime do so to save their lives and because of fear of shame." For those who kill their children because these would be a hindrance to the continuation of their life of vice, he favored the retention of the "poena culei," that is, drowning in a sack accompanied by animals.

Then Christian Thomasius, a professor in the University of Leipzig, asserted that "legal science should be grounded rather on man's moral nature than on biblical tradition." The theologians of course would not stand for that and so proceeded to make it too hot for him. He then went to the University of Halle. But two heads took the place of the one that had been eliminated. Wolff and Leibnitz set up the rule that "everything is right and permissible which seems necessary for the attainment of public tranquility and safety."[56]

Frederick the Great followed in the footsteps of these men. He put into practice two important preachments of his. The first was expressed in a letter to Voltaire: "I believed . . . that it would be better to seek out causes and prevent crimes than to punish them."[57] And the second was expressed

[56] For the quotation from Leyser see Wehrli, "Der Kindsmord, etc.," p. 38; from Thomasius see Calvin Thomas, "A History of German Literature." New York, 1909, p. 202f.; for a discussion of the theories of Wolff and Leibnitz see Ferdinand Willensbücher, "Die strafrechtsphilosophischen Anschauungen Friedrichs des Grossen." Breslau, 1904, p. 63.

[57] See Willensbücher, loc. cit., p. 17.

in an essay: "Natural equity demands that there should be proportion between the crime and its punishment."[58] These two principles were the origin of a new theory of punishment, the prophylactic. This involved the principle that by prophylactic activity the causes of crimes could be discovered and the crimes themselves prevented.

Accordingly Frederick the Great and his contemporaries opened attack on three evils which were causes of infanticide: indefiniteness of the law, cruelty of punishment, especially in the execution of it, and arbitrariness of judges. In the year of his coronation Frederick decreed that the punishment of sacking, which his father had only recently reinstated, should be abolished. All infanticides should thereafter be punished by decapitation.[59] To avoid all judicial arbitrariness he decreed that all criminal findings should be sent directly to him. When on June 26, 1743, his advisers urged that this revision would require too much of his time he answered in very emphatic German: "No! All criminal decrees shall be sent to me, otherwise all kinds of abuses will come into existence and the people in the provinces can be hoodwinked at pleasure."[60] On June 20, 1746, Frederick abolished church penance in all the churches of his kingdom, "because the punishment of the sins of the flesh and the consequent disgrace give occasion for infanticide, . . . and because it serves rather to increase resentment and bitterness than to produce betterment."[60]

In his "Dissertation sur les raisons d'établir ou d'abroger les lois" he again devotes much space to a discussion of the evil of infanticide. "Is there any ultimate good in the manner in which we punish infanticides?," he asks after reviewing the practice among primitive peoples. "Heaven knows that I do not for a moment excuse this horrible act of these Medeas who, cruel to themselves and to the voice of blood, kill the future race. But I would that the reader might weigh all the prejudices of custom and deign to give some attention to

[58] *Idem*, p. 19.

[59] The decree was dated July 31, 1740. It is available in Mylius: "Corpus Constitutionem Marchicarum, etc."

[60] See J. D. E. Preuss, "Friedrich der Grosse." Berlin, 1832, I, 337.

the reflections that I am going to present. The laws, do they
not attach infamy to clandestine child-birth? A girl only too
easily fooled by the promises of a seducer, does she not find
herself compelled by the very force of circumstances, to choose
between the loss of her honor and the elimination of the unhappy fruit that she has conceived? Is it not the fault of the
laws to place a girl in such a desperate position? And does
not the severity of the judges deprive the state of two subjects,
the child which it forces the mother to kill, and then the mother
herself in expiation of her crime, a mother who may have intended to make it possible to repair her loss by becoming a
legal mother and then to propagate legally? I know that
they save an innumerable number of bastards to society,
but would it not be better to take the evil by the roots and
save all of these poor creatures who perish miserably, by
abolishing the detriments attached to the results of an im-
prudent and secret love?"[61]

And then there are two edicts devoted entirely to an attempt
to prevent the delict by actively eliminating the causes.
One was issued August 17, 1756, and was entitled "Edikt zur
Verhütung des Kindesmords," the other February 8, 1765,
entitled "Edikt wider den Mord neugebohrner unehelicher
Kinder, Verheimlichung der Schwangerschaft, und Nieder-
kunft." In both decrees the intention of the king is evident.
He tried to make it possible for every unmarried mother to
come within the law, his concern being rather to save both
mother and child than to lose both or to make them unde-
sirable members of society. It is particularly interesting to
note that he wanted mother and child to remain together.
He instructed unmarried mothers to report their condition to
any married mother, who in turn was obliged to assist her in
every way possible; or, if she preferred, to report her condition
to the local authorities, who should provide for her. If she
complied with this requirement no punishment whatever
would be inflicted. Parents and employers of girls were forbidden to flog pregnant unmarried girls. They were also
forbidden to discharge such girls without providing them with

[61] Cf. "Oeuvres de Frédéric le Grand." IX, 30f.

means for their sustenance or until they had notified the local authorities. The seducer of the girl was instructed to provide and care for her whom he had got with child, provided she notified him of the fact. Parents of girls who were about to become mothers before marriage were forbidden to treat their children harshly under heavy penalty.

Frederick was so intent on eradicating causes that he even attacked the church in its assertion that only those marriages which it sanctioned were legal. When it was reported to him that a certain divine refused to marry a couple because the man wished to marry his father's brother's wife, "because such marriages were expressly forbidden in the Word of God," Frederick instructed: "If they (the Divines) do not want to marry him, let the couple go to the council house, make their contract as they do in Holland, and I shall declare their children legal."

While Frederick was on the right track in trying to seek out the causes of infanticide and to eradicate them, he failed to discover one very important cause—the insistence that his soldiery should remain unmarried. In the last years of his life he discovered this and immediately began correcting this evil by instituting soldier marriages or encouraging ordinary marriage among his soldiers, but this came so late in his life that it did not affect the fact that after the Seven Years' War he could assert in his edict of 1765 that infanticide had become more frequent than ever. The reason was to be found in the quartering of a large army on the people of his kingdom, an army of men who were required to remain unmarried.

Frederick's activities in regard to this problem were paralleled by those of Maria Theresa, empress of Austria, together with those of Joseph II, who succeeded her. She abolished torture in 1775, established maternity and foundling houses, and later abolished capital punishment. So too Catherine II, empress of Russia, immediately upon her coronation founded poor and foundling houses. In order to improve the defective legal procedure she appointed a commission to draw up a new code of laws. Whole passages of this code were literally copied from Beccaria, the eminent Italian criminologist. She also abolished torture and capital punishment.

And then there was Beccaria just referred to. In his famous "Essay on Crimes and Punishment"[62] he asserted that the penalty of death was not authorized by any right, for no such right existed. It was further neither necessary nor useful. Of the unmarried mother he said: "The murder of bastard children is the effect of a cruel dilemma, in which a woman finds herself when she has been seduced through weakness or overcome by force. The alternative is, either her own infamy or the death of a being who is incapable of feeling the loss of life. How can she avoid preferring the latter to the inevitable misery of herself and her unhappy infant? The best method of preventing this crime, would be effectively to protect the weak woman from that tyranny which exaggerates all vices that cannot be concealed under the cloak of virtue. I do not seek to lessen that just abhorrence which these crimes deserve, but to discover the sources from whence they spring; and I think I may draw the following conclusion: That the punishment of a crime cannot be just if the laws have not endeavored to prevent that crime by the best means which times and circumstances allow." Voltaire wrote a commentary for the translation. It was headed: "The Occasion of this Commentary." In it he tells how with infinite satisfaction he had read Beccaria's book. Then he continues: "I flattered myself that it would be a means of softening the remnants of barbarism in the laws of many nations; I hoped for some reformation in mankind, when I was informed that, within a few miles of my abode, they had just hanged a girl of eighteen, beautiful, well-formed, accomplished, and of a very reputable family." He then proceeds to tell the history of the case, and of the trial and the execution of this girl, who was an infanticide.

In the activities of Frederick the Great, of Maria Theresa, of Catherine II, of Beccaria, Voltaire, Montesquieu and their

[62] "Dei Delitti e delle Pene," 1764. Within 18 months, six editions were sold. Translated into French by Morellet in 1766, into English in 1768, into German in 1764.

adherents, was the tinder which was destined to kindle the greatest revolt against antiquated laws and customs that Europe has ever experienced. In Germany it was a period of Storm and Stress, of passionate revolt against outworn conventions in art, and against hoary social abuses intrenched in law and custom.

CHAPTER II

THE HUMANITARIAN REVOLT OF THE EIGHTEENTH CENTURY

Led by Frederick the Great and his contemporaries, the exponents of the Age of Enlightenment, the writers of the last three decades of the eighteenth century turned their attention to the discovery and elimination of the causes of unmarried motherhood and consequent infanticide rather than to devising means of punishing it.

Foremost among the causes of so much illegitimacy was the amazing prevalence of prostitution, which went hand in hand with a constant decrease in the number of marriages and an increase of infanticide. One of the contestants for the Mannheim prize suggested that the question should read: "not how can infanticide be prevented, but which are the best means to stop prostitution?"[1] Lenz in his essay "Ueber die Soldatenehen" severely scored the attempts to punish illegitimate sexual commerce, for that would only result in "a concealment of sexual irregularities and a consequent inability to judge its dangerousness." "These destructive habits," he wrote, "enervate citizens and soldiers, marriages are becoming rare, and our progeny is miserably poor."[2] List in his contest essay asserted that "in our days prostitution is the fashionable vice," and a poem in the *Deutsches Museum* expresses the same opinion. Part of it runs

> Ob du junger Unschuld Kränze raubst,
> Dir Betrug und Ehebruch erlaubst,
> Ob dich heimlich Neid und Hochmut quälen,
> Das entehrt dich Erstgebornen nicht;
> Denn die Mode duldet schwarze Seelen,
> Aber keine Flecken im Gesicht.[3]

[1] See *Allgemeine Deutsche Bibliothek*, 85, 156f.

[2] Jakob Michael Reinhold Lenz, "Ueber die Soldatenehen. Nach der Handschrift der Berliner Königlichen Bibliothek zum ersten Male herausgegeben von Karl Freye." Leipzig, 1914, p. 22f.

[3] *Deutsches Museum*, 1776², p. 601ff., "Die Mode," signed Ue.

Cella in a discourse "Von Errichtung öffentlicher Bordelle oder Hurenwirtschaften in grossen Städten und auf Universitäten" gives an excellent picture of the status of morals at a large German university of that time. "I know very certainly," he says, "and anyone who will investigate will bear me out, that at most universities at the beginning of each half year, when new students arrive, at least a third of the number is in the care of physicians and army surgeons, to be cured of their fashionable diseases of gallantry."[4]

This widespread prevalence of illegitimacy was due to many causes. Laziness and idleness seem to have been rife among all classes. The inflated prosperity which followed the Seven Years' War was mostly to blame. J. G. Schlosser insists that the girls were "fickle, voluptuous, lazy, prattling. They are surrounded in the city by many soldiers and officers who have nothing to do but to drill a few hours each day. Idleness and luxury alone are the sources of prostitution."[5] Iselin records the offer of a prize for the best essay on the question: "What are the most practicable and efficacious means to improve the mind and heart as well as the morals of the common man in the towns and country, and especially how can he be encouraged and accustomed to diligence and industry?"[6] Christian Wilhelm Kindleben in his "Studentenlexicon" defines the word "arbeitsam": "an epithet which was formerly applied to the peasant, if one wanted to flatter him. . . . Now the peasant seems to be ashamed of this name and at public meetings and elsewhere insists that he be called 'lieber Ehrengeachteter.' O tempora! O mores!"[7]

A show of supposed wealth or luxury always accompanies laziness. It was natural, therefore, that one Mannheim contestant should suggest that a "diminution of luxury" would

---

[4] "Johann Jakob Cella's freymüthige Aufsätze." Anspach, 1784, p. 53f.

[5] Johann Georg Schlosser, "Die Wudbianer, Eine nicht gekrönte Preiss-Schrift über die Frage: Wie ist der Kindermord zu verhindern ohne die Unzucht zu befördern?" Basel, 1785. In "Kleine Schriften," IV, p. 18.

[6] Isaak Iselin, in IX of *Ephemeriden der Menschheit oder Bibliothek der Sittenlehre, der Politik und der Gesetzgebung.* Basel, 1777, p. 124.

[7] Halle, 1781. No. 7 in "Bibliothek litterarischer und culturhistorischer Seltenheiten." Leipzig, 1899, p. 17.

eliminate much illegitimacy.[8] Hamann lamented: "O dead and unproductive prosperity, sanctimonious Pharisee of our century!"[9] List in his essay exclaimed: "O accursed luxury! the most beautiful of feminine virtues would be destroyed much less often without thee. Monarchs! ye who are able to eradicate this evil, use every energy to root out this curse." Lenz in his "Zerbin" attributes the almost successful concealment of infanticide by Marie to the pockets which girls of the lower classes wore in their dresses, thus making it easy to conceal their pregnant condition.[10] Hermes therefore recommended a very plain suit, similar to that worn by the early Greeks, which should take the place of women's skirts and bodices, in order in this way to remove everything which might conceal the physical changes of the body and make infanticide an impossibility because pregnancy would be detected in the first months of its progress.[11] Goethe very well knew the weakness of the girls of his time when he made Faust appeal to the fancy of Gretchen by giving her a casket of jewels, which she paraded at the house of neighbor Martha.

> Nach Golde drängt,
> Am Golde hängt
> Doch alles. Ach wir Armen!

Then there was an unusual emigration from country to city, and that always increases illegitimacy. Country girls, who had little experience with the ways of the world, became easy victims of young men who had had years of training in seduction. Pestalozzi devotes one whole section of his essay to a discussion of the circumstances which usually brought

[8] See *Allgemeine Deutsche Bibliothek*, 54, 111. Cf. also *Idem*, 52, 478. There are also many cursory discussions of the evil effects of luxury. See Johann Timotheus Hermes, "Sophiens Reise von Memel nach Sachsen." Leipzig, 1776, I, 620; N. E. Tscharner, "Ueber die Nothwendigkeit der Prachtgesetze in einem Freystaate," in *Berlinische Monatsschrift*, 1769.

[9] Hamanns Schriften. Berlin, 1823, IV, 231.

[10] Jakob Michael Reinhold Lenz, "Gesammelte Schriften." Herausgegeben von Ludwig Tieck. Berlin, 1828, III, 165.

[11] Cf. Konstantin Muskalla, "Johann Timotheus Hermes, Ein Beitrag zur Kultur- und Literaturgeschichte des achtzehnten Jahrhunderts." Breslau, 1910, p. 29. Iselin too had some pertinent things to suggest on the manner of dress, cf. "Palämon oder von der Ueppigkeit." Zürich, 1769, p. 26.

about the large number of infanticides among servant girls, who generally came from the country. Among the causes enumerated are these: The wanton attitude of their superiors spoils the girls' innocence. City food and drink and even city work intensify the sexual instinct of country girls. Traps of seduction and unfaithfulness are only play and pastime on the part of city men. The laws seem to be made to heap on such girls all the blame and punishment for any sexual irregularity, the disadvantage of these girls consisting in their ignorance of the crooked high-ways and by-ways of legal procedure, while these are known to their seducers. Pestalozzi concludes the section by asserting that the history of the crime proved that most infanticides are committed by servant girls under these unfavorable conditions.[12]

Games in which kissing played a part seem to have been common also. Thümmel in "Die Reise in die mittäglichen Provinzen von Frankreich" gives a description of a beautiful girl who had become insane because her seducer had deserted her after she became a prospective mother. She attributes her fall to such games of kissing.

> Da setzte mir die Zeit des Pfandspiels und der Küsse
> Ans Ohr ein Räuberheer, das immer lauter rief:
> Welch Mädchen! Gott, wie süsse
> Und wie naiv![13]

We get an excellent idea of the extent of this custom among young people from Goethe's experience with Friederike Brion. He tells us in "Dichtung und Wahrheit" how careful he had been not to kiss a girl since his experience with the daughters of his dancing-master in Strassburg. "I carefully evaded every desire which prompts a young man to win this more or less valuable favor from a charming girl. But even in the most respectable company I was put to a very uncomfortable test. Just those more or less clever games which young people

---

[12] See "Ueber Gesetzgebung und Kindermord," p. 418f. J. G. Schlosser also refers to certain games and means of introduction which assisted would-be seducers of servant girls. See "Kleine Schriften," IV, 19.

[13] "August Moritz von Thümmels sämmtliche Werke." Leipzig, 1839, VI, 23f.

like to play, were founded on pawns for the release of which kisses have no small value."[14]   He later admits that the friends who tried in vain for a long time to get him to kiss Friederike, finally succeeded.

Masked balls and nocturnal dances also furnished an excellent opportunity for young men trained in seduction to lead girls astray.   List asserted that the dancing-schools of his day were homes of sexual vice.   Rabener, long before the storm broke, objected to masked balls.   Heinrich Leopold Wagner took particular delight in scoring these evils.   In "Die Kindermörderinn" Humbrecht, the father of Evchen, explains to the Magister that he has no objection to dances in themselves: "let those dance there who belong there—who objects?   For the men and women of the nobility, for the squires and ladies, who because of all their distinction do not know what to do with the good Lord's time, for them it may be pleasure—who has anything against it?   But wives of artisans, daughters of civilians, shall keep their noses out of it; they can wear out enough shoes at weddings, academic banquets and such things, they do not need to gamble on their honor and good name. . . . Especially if a sugar-sweet lad in uniform, or a little baron—God have mercy on them— takes a girl of our class to such places, then one can bet ten to one that he will not bring her back home as he got her."

The kind of literature read and the type of plays produced at the theaters were also incentives to an increase of sexual irregularities.   Seduction had a veritable heyday in Europe when the literature of sentimentalism reached its zenith. Czerny remarks: "The esthetic value of these works is in the main very small: they are of much greater interest to the historian of civilization than to the historian of literature."[15] Jean Paul in the fourth chapter of his "Grönländische Prozesse oder satirische Skizzen," having previously made an attempt to trace the effects of sentimentalism on real life, says: "Let us return to our attempt to depict sentimentalism from the angle which has been decried too much, and try to convince

---

[14] Dritter Theil.   Elftes Buch.   Weimarer Ausgabe, 28, p. 13.
[15] J. Czerny, "Sterne, Hippel und Jean Paul."   Berlin, 1904, p. 18.

the fair sex that it is still to its advantage to weep as much now as before. The most noted thing for which sentimentalism can be recommended and which we now repeat, is undoubtedly this, that it promotes marriage, especially pre-nuptial marriages (Vor-Ehen). Like circumcision, it has not only hallowed the souls but has increased the number of physical bodies, and both are equally useful for this world as for heaven. The arithmetical proof for this assertion we will leave to a second Süssmilch, to whom we here refer."[16]

Eisenhardt in Lenz's "Die Soldaten," who is really the moralist Lenz himself, rebukes the officers for favoring the type of plays produced at the theaters. "The grossest crimes against the most sacred rights of fathers and families are portrayed in the most alluring colors. . . . To deceive a vigilant father, or to instruct an innocent girl in vice, these are the plots which are presented." To this one of the officers replies: "Oh, pshaw! is it always and forever necessary to be learning something at the theater? We simply amuse ourselves, is not that enough?" Eisenhardt answers: "Would to heaven that you only amused yourself and that you did not learn! As it is you imitate what is performed and you bring misfortune and curses to the homes of honest families."

The best epitomization of the status of the sex problem during the last half of the eighteenth century is given by Schubart in his "Leben und Gesinnungen." He says: "The Germans were formerly distinguished above all peoples, as Tacitus long ago remarked, for strict chastity. . . . But now— how little is golden chastity valued by us! Our unnatural mimicry of the French has introduced all kinds of frivolities among us, has weakened our stamina, and degraded us so far that we only smile at prostitution and adultery. Yes, we seem to bend all our energies to the end of spoiling our children early in life. We teach them to sing songs of loving and kiss-

[16] Süssmilch was statistician at the court of Frederick the Great and showed much concern about the increasing number of illegitimate children. For other expressions on the detrimental element in the literature of sentimentalism, cf. Schlosser, "Kleine Schriften," IV, 20; "Christian Friedrich Daniel Schubart's des Patrioten gesammelte Schriften und Schicksale." Stuttgart, 1839, I, 162f.; Gustav Freytag, "Bilder aus der deutschen Vergangenheit." Leipzig, 1882, III, 98 and 349.

ing, we do not restrain ourselves in their presence, we take
them to the most vicious plays, where the most immoral transgressions of voluptuousness, where perjury and adultery,
seduction and the ruination of innocence and virtue are called
mere gallantry, real life—yes, even Enlightenment. 'On the
downy pillows of voluptuousness,' says Young, 'many a kingdom has gone to sleep!' Will you fare better, my fatherland?
. . . The morals here and in Mannheim are quite loose. . . .
Prostitution and adultery are fashionable sins, which one, it
is true, confesses, but immediately commits again. To keep
a mistress is here, as in Paris, London, Berlin, good taste.
Voluptuousness has her temples, priests and priestesses, here as
everywhere. O, ancient German chastity, where art thou?"[17]

But all these causes of illegitimacy were only immediate
results of the real root of the whole trouble, the scarcity of
marriages. Kreuzfeld in his prize essay points out that "the
fewer marriages there are, the more illegitimate sexual relations, the more illegitimate children, the more infanticides."[18]
Pestalozzi spoke of his day as "the marriageless age." "The
hosts of the unmarried," he asserts, "yield without restraint
to all the allurements of their sexual needs . . . and no power
of honor or protective national morality can stop the destruction of our country. The starting point of all human degrada-
tion is hardness of heart; and the simple satisfaction of the sex
impulse leads immeasurably less to that than does forced
subjugation and crooked evasion of natural sexual intercourse.
Our public morals and laws seem to have been made for the
sole purpose of hardening the heart."[19]

Who were these hosts of the unmarried? First of all the
soldiers, who were compelled to remain unmarried.

> Wer sich in preussischen Dienst will begeben,
>   Der muss sich sein Lebtag kein Weibchen nicht nehmen:
>   Er muss sich nicht fürchten vor Hagel und Wind,
>   Beständig verbleiben und bleiben geschwind.[20]

[17] "Gesammelte Schriften," I, 114ff., 162f.
[18] In "Drei Preisschriften, etc.," p. 144.
[19] In the above mentioned essay, pp. 385, 425.
[20] "Husarenbraut. Fliegendes Blatt aus dem siebenjährigen Kriege."
See "Des Knaben Wunderhorn," I, 189.

All the ruling princes of that time believed that a single man was a better soldier than a married one. Laukhard, upon his return from a trip to the Prussian army in Champagne, wrote of the terrible corruption of morals existing everywhere that soldiers were quartered. "Of the terrible corruption of morals," he writes, "which the French emigrants have brought to pass in Germany, I too have been a witness. In Koblenz an old subaltern officer from Trier told me that from the age of twelve on there was not a single maiden, the damned Frenchmen had made every girl far and wide a prostitute. And so it was, all the girls and women, even many old nuns not excepted, were intolerably flirtatious. One merchant's daughter confessed openly that she had sold her chastity for six carolins to a Frenchman. No, so spoiled our German girls never were! And as it was in Koblenz, so it was everywhere where these emigrants have come."[21]

Friedrich Rudolph Salzmann reports that in Strassburg "every peasant home is closed to the officers of the garrison, because one fears ill reports!"[22] List asserts that soldiers caused frightful devastation, both moral and physical, among the common people.[23] Schlosser admits that wherever the soldier was stationed, there civilian freedom was impossible,[24] and a contributor to Schlözer's *Stats-Anzeigen* called soldiers "hired mercenaries of the state, who destroy good morals."[25]

This then accounts for the frequent delineation of the soldier as the seducer of innocent girls. Lenz's "Die Soldaten" is perhaps the most striking example. In Act III, scene 4, of this drama Eisenhardt exclaims: "O militarism, terrible unmarried state, what caricatures you make of human beings!" Lenz's attitude was not merely a revolt against the soldiers' sexual transgressions; by personal experience he had come to believe that something had to be done to make it possible for the soldier to satisfy his sexual needs. He had this in mind

[21] Johannes Scherr, "Deutsche Kultur- und Sittengeschichte." Leipzig, 1873, p. 473f.
[22] See Johann Froitzheim, "Goethe und Heinrich Leopold Wagner," p. 48f.
[23] List, "Ueber Hurerey und Kindermord," p. 56f.
[24] Schlosser, "Kleine Schriften," IV, p. 240f.
[25] XI, 470. Cf. also Muskalla, "J. T. Hermes," p. 29.

when the Countess La Roche expounds to Marie, the victim of
the soldier Desportes, that the "soldier ceases to be a good
soldier as soon as he becomes a good lover, for he has sworn
on oath to the king that he will not be a lover and permits the
king to pay him for it." In the last scene of the drama the
colonel reports that a citizen of the fatherland with his whole
family has been dashed into irremediable destruction. The
countess frankly asserts that it is the "result of the unmarried
state of our soldiery." The colonel asks: "How shall we get
rid of this evil? Even Homer asserted that a good husband
and father was a poor soldier, and experience proves it. . . . I
look upon the soldier as a monster to whom from time to time
an unfortunate young woman must be willingly sacrificed, in
order that other wives and daughters may be spared. . . .
There should be established by the king endowed institutions
for soldier-wives, where young girls might sacrifice their lives
to the good of the state."

To this latter recommendation Herder objected. In his
answer Lenz suggests that "as far as the last scene is concerned, I think all aggravating difficulties might be solved
by leaving out or changing a few expressions of the colonel,
e. g., that about the concubines, might be left out entirely,
and the colonel could speak of soldiers' wives, who, like the
national guard, would be selected by lot in all the villages and
then, like the Roman women, who were called *conferreatæ*,
they could marry for a definite period of years. The king
would rear the children, the girls would later go back to their
home villages at the expiration of their term and would remain
honorable." To these suggestions Lenz added further that
real soldier-marriages did not seem to him feasible. He
must have changed his mind soon thereafter, for in his essay
"Ueber die Soldatenehen" he ardently favors them. From
the introduction to this essay we learn too that Lenz actually
planned to carry out Herder's suggestion in regard to the last
scene of the drama, but the changes were never printed.

Perhaps Lenz so speedily changed his mind because public
opinion was so strongly in favor of soldier-marriages. Hermes
in "Sophiens Reise von Memel nach Sachsen" lets Puff make

the following recommendations: "I would give the soldier a few more pfennings per day, and then he would have to marry. Now he satisfies his desires on that which he can get by stealth from the other sex, consequently he becomes beggarish, has an un-German mind and is thievish. These married soldiers would have a large progeny, consequently the enlistment of foreign soldiers would cease; love for the fatherland and fidelity to the army would return gradually, and the invasion of foreign vices would be stopped. More than that, the married soldier would be active, healthy, and because he goes to battle for wife and child, he would again become what the German formerly was, a 'Brafkerl'."[26]

This idea of soldier-marriages found such universal favor that even Möser admitted that the adoption of the English plan of pseudo-marriage would be preferable to existing conditions. The English at that time did not permit unmarried women to follow in the wake of the army. Instead their soldiers were permitted to take a woman to wife before the drum and in the same manner part from her again. "English officers have assured me," Möser says in his essay "Von den Militär-Ehen der Engländer," "that there is more jealousy on the part of soldiers for such a wife than one finds in Christian marriage. . . . Moreover the Englishman loves to be a father, therefore it seldom happens that he deserts a woman whom he has impregnated or fails to care for his child."[27]

[26] I, 619f. The passage as quoted by Muskalla, in his "Johann Timotheus Hermes," p. 27f., unless the edition used was very different from the one I used, is copied incorrectly. I was not able to get the edition he used and could therefore not compare. The suspicion that it was copied incorrectly is confirmed by two other references on the same page, both of which are incorrect. The reference to Rachel, 4 Satyra, p. 43, Hallenser Neudrucke 200/202, should read

Der Raben Mutter sucht am Galgen ihr Gewinn,
Und trägt das blutig Aass den kalen Jungen hin.

The difference between "der Raben Mutter" and "die Rabenmutter," as Muskalla has it, and between "kalen" and "kalten," change the force of the passage so that it can not possibly be said that infanticide was referred to. The other reference is to Joseph Hansen, "Zauberwahn, Inquisition und Hexenprozess im Mittelalter." München und Leipzig, 1900. The reference to chap. 31 is an impossibility for there are only 6 chapters.

[27] "Justus Möser's sämmtliche Werke." Berlin und Stettin, 1798, IV, 23f. Cf. also Pfeil, "Drei Preisschriften," p. 58; Hess, "Freymüthige Gedanken," p. 384f.; Hippel, "Sämmtliche Werke," V, 248f.

Rector Stuve made one of those fantastic recommendations which one finds so plentifully during this period. "How would it be," he writes in an article entitled "Nachrichten von der Frankfurtischen Garnisonschule, nebst Vorschlägen über die Soldatenehen," "if all inmates of cloisters and convents were given permission to marry officers of the army? How many poor girls would be saved from this absolutely injudicious cloister life! How many could thus be helped to husbands! How many heroic officers would thus obtain wives!"[28]

Nowhere was the subject of soldier-marriages threshed out more thoroughly than in Lenz's "Ueber die Soldatenehen," which was written in 1776, begun as early as 1773, but not published until 1914. "The dire results of the unmarried state of the soldiers are without number, and only an enemy of mankind would recount all of them. . . . How many disrupted marriages, how many deserted girls, how many harlots so dangerous to the population, how many other horrible effects, infanticide, thefts, poisonings—industry has ceased, . . . the arts are no longer practiced . . . where is the cause?" He refers the reader to an account of soldier life by a certain Hollander Steenkerk of Leipzig, being still unwilling to have it known that he was the author of "Die Soldaten."

"What should the soldier fight for?" Lenz asks. "For the king, for the fatherland? No. Prosperity and self-defence are the real things for which a soldier should fight. O, ye rulers! are ye so unacquainted with human nature, not to feel in its whole force what new life, what wonderful power would course in the veins of your soldiers if they fought for wives and children?"[29] Then Lenz proceeds to outline his plan of soldier-marriages. Every soldier must be citizen first of all. Half of his time shall be spent in the army, the other half at home with his family. He could never be happier than when he is with his wife who awaits him, with his children who work for him. And during the six months of active service he would work like a beaver, thinking always of protecting his loved ones rather than of planning sexual excesses.

[28] *Berlinische Monatsschrift*, V, 213f.
[29] "Ueber die Soldatenehen," p. 45f.

"And if war should come would he not fight like a lion? Would he yield to a bloodthirsty enemy who stood before him, ready to rape his wife and kill his children?"[30]

The whole object of his essay is to restore good morals in society and to do away with that just hatred which existed between soldiers and citizens. The soldier, before whom every father trembled for his daughters, every husband for his wife, would again stand in public favor, and instead of being a curse to humanity he would become a blessing.

Laukhard did not approve of this sentiment favorable to soldier-marriages. He had seen such marriages in Halle and did not get a very good impression of them. He asserted that these marriages were usually unhappy and the children, if there were any, were of small value to the state because of defective rearing.

Another group of men who remained unmarried, for a time at least, were the students. Cella in the essay referred to above recommended the establishment of public institutions where girls might sacrifice themselves to the sexual needs of these men, so that all other girls could retain their virtue. Still another group that played havoc with public morals and destroyed the happiness of many homes were private tutors (Hofmeister). Lenz's "Der Hofmeister" is the most striking literary treatment. Here Läuffer, a private tutor, seduces Gustchen, a mixture of sentimentalism and stupidity. She flees to hide her condition, but is later found by her father and brought back to the paternal home. Fritzchen, the fruit of the forbidden relationship, is adopted by Fritz von Berg, Gustchen's fiancé, she herself is generously forgiven and taken to wife. In the last scene of the drama Fritz von Berg takes the child in his arms, kisses it and exclaims: "This child is mine too; a sad witness of the weakness of your sex and the stupidity of ours, most of all of the advantageous education of young girls by tutors. . . . And still infinitely precious to me, because it is the picture of its mother. At any rate, my sweet boy! I shall never have you educated by a tutor."

The history of the tutor and his influence is of course con-

[30] *Idem*, p. 32f.

nected more or less with Rousseau's "La nouvelle Héloise,"
in which St. Preux plays the rôle of the seducer. Arnim was
right in taking this influence into consideration in his "Ver-
kleidungen des französischen Hofmeisters und seine deutschen
Zöglinge."

More important than these types of seducers was the representative of the nobility, who preyed on the girls of the lower
classes. It is important to note that this type met with very
severe criticism by imaginative writers, while there are comparatively few references to it in other literature. The explanation can probably be found in the fact that other writers
were unable to publish any polemic against the ruling class.
With poets, novelists and playwrights it was quite different.
Their allusions were only indirect and they could always hide
behind the cloak of poetic license.

Linguet, an eminent French criminologist, opposed the
abolition of capital punishment mainly on the ground that
there would then be no means of holding the nobility in check
in their ravages among innocent girls. Hebel tells of a very
interesting method of punishing a young baron, who in a city
of twenty thousand houses led astray all the virtuous girls.
"Many a tear witnessed against him, many a marriage and
family had been deprived of their peace and happiness, and
he always laughed at what he had done." So the citizens of
the city formed a sort of Ku Klux Klan, which took the baron
prisoner one night, led him to a distant place, there held court
and condemned him to die. The execution was postponed to
the next night, thus giving the baron plenty of time to reflect
on his past life. The following night instead of executing
him, they took him back to his home. He never again attempted to follow his former course.[31]

In the poetry of the period a number of customs of these
knights of the nobility are revealed. Writers took particular
delight in ridiculing the knight who sent out a squire to find
him a bed-fellow. Uz in a poem called "Die alten und heutigen deutschen Sitten" compares the knight of old to his
modern successor:

[31] "Hebel's Werke," "Deutsche Nationallitteratur," 142, II, 292.

> Dass stets der kühne Junker jagte,
> Auch eh' es auf den Bergen tagte,
> Hiess ihnen Streitbarkeit,
> Noch jagt und schmaust er um die Wette,
> Indess besorgt ein Freund sein Bette,
> Zu unsrer Zeit.[32]

Friedrich Graf zu Stolberg in his poem "Ritter Bayard, genant der Ritter sonder Furcht und Tadel" tells of another such voluptuous knight:

> Einst, als er glühte von dem Becher,
> Und um ihn her
> erscholl der Rundgesang der Zecher,
> da sandt' er seiner Knappen einen aus,
> der trat in ein verarmtes Haus.

Here he finds a daughter, who is led away. The mother follows and finally through her entreaties succeeds in persuading the knight to forego the seduction of Dortchen. The poem ends in a paean of praise for the knight and all others who do like him.[33]

The folk-song "Vom Grafen und der Magd" is reproduced in an endless variety of ways. In its simplest form it is the story of a count who seduces a girl of the lower classes and then when she is a prospective mother, deserts her. The girl later dies either before or in child-birth. Generally infanticide is merely suggested. So it is for instance in the version which Goethe sent to Herder, when the latter was collecting folk-songs. The mother of the girl when she discovers that the daughter has been seduced and is pregnant says:

> Seyd still seyd still liebe Tochter mein,
> Der Reden seyd ihr stille.
> Wenn wir das Kindlein geboren han
> So wollen wir's lernen schwimmen.

The girl dies before the child is born, the count returns too late, and stabs himself with his shining sword.

---

[32] " Bibliothek der deutschen Klassiker," IV, 564f.
[33] *Deutsches Museum*, 1782[1], p. 68f.

The extant versions of this folk-song and the direct utiliza-
tions of the theme it contains have recently been compiled
and discussed by Rudolf Thietz in "Die Ballade vom Grafen
und der Magd. Ein Rekonstruktionsversuch und Beitrag
zur Charakterisierung der Volkspoesie."[34] The assertion that
this ballad is a real folk-song may be accepted, but certainly
the English ballad in Percy's collection entitled "Childe
Waters" ought to be considered in determining the origin and
development. It is not at all impossible that the German folk-
song is only one of a much larger number of versions among
many other peoples, or it might be possible to trace all the
versions in Germany back to the English ballad. Why
Bürger's poems "Der Ritter und sein Liebchen" and "Des
Pfarrers Tochter von Taubenhain" were not counted among
the direct variations of this ballad, is not clear to me. That
Bürger was interested in Percy's "relique" is evidenced by his
translation of the English poem under the title "Graf Walter.
Nach dem Alt-Englischen." The first of this trio of poems
may be looked upon as the embryonic form of "Des Pfarrers
Tochter von Taubenhain." It tells the story of a knight who
is about to depart for war. He bids adieu to the girl he has
got with child. Upon her wish that he may soon return to
claim her as his bride he laughs.

> Drauf ritt der Ritter hop sa sa!
> Und strich sein Bärtchen trallala!
> Sein Liebchen sah ihn reiten,
> Und hörte noch von weiten
> Sein Lachen ha ha ha!

A reader of Percy's ballad cannot fail to detect the similarity.
The most artistic treatment of the theme is to be found in
Heinrich von Kleist's "Das Käthchen von Heilbronn."[35]
This drama follows Percy's ballad more closely in utilizing

---

[34] Strassburg, 1913. See Vol. 119 of "Quellen und Forschungen zur Sprach-
und Culturgeschichte der germanischen Völker." Goethe's poem is entitled
"Das Lied vom Herren und der Magd." See *Der junge Goethe*, ed. 2, II, 68f.

[35] "Gottfried August Bürgers sämmtliche Werke." Göttingen, 1829, I, p.
132f.: Der Ritter und sein Liebchen; II, 29: Des Pfarrers Tochter von Taubenhain; II, 142f.: Graf Walter.

the same happy solution, instead of permitting the affair to end in a tragedy:

O nun, o nun, süss süsse Maid,
Süss süsse Maid, halt' ein!
Es soll ja Tauf' und Hochzeit nun
In Einer Stunde seyn.

There was written during this period a veritable flood of literature in which the difference of social rank (Standesunterschied) plays an important rôle, but the consideration of this lies outside of this research.

These, then, were the hosts of the unmarried. It is no wonder that the problem of marriage was discussed by men of every class. There were two opinions. There were those that favored doing away with the public disgrace which attached to illegitimate sexual relations and a return to the natural state, as nearly as that was possible. But the other opinion, and it was held by the majority, favored doing away with all obstacles to legal marriage, and urged the specific encouragement of such marriages. Hippel introduced the slogan: "Go into the marriage cloister!" although he himself was a bachelor for life. That was the burden of his whole message in his essay "Ueber die Ehe." "The thermometer of morality always has been matrimony," he asserted, "as it was with the number of marriages, so stood the stocks and bonds of public morals!"[36] The old assertion that the sole object of marriage was the propagation and rearing of children was attacked especially by Kant. He did not wish to oppose marriage, but wanted to make of it an institution in harmony with Pure Reason.[37] Hamann was inclined to be more conservative still and sided with Möser and others in defending absolute state rights and denying that natural rights entered into the question.[38] Herr Deutsch and Puff in Hermes' "Sophiens Reise von Memel nach Sachsen" have a long debate on the merits of legal marriage and on the proper defini-

[36] "Sämmtliche Werke," V, 24.
[37] "Sämmtliche Werke," Leipzig, 1867, VII, 149f.
[38] "Hamann's Schriften." Herausgegeben von Friedrich Roth zu Berlin. 1824, IV, 223f.

tion of adultery. The object of Hermes was evidently to preach that adultery could be prevented if each individual would guarantee his own virtue by not destroying the chastity of others. He further penetrated to the crux of the whole problem by insisting that seduction and desertion were due to masculine and not feminine vice, that a woman never becomes a harlot willingly, but only because some man has in the first instance made her be one. The day was coming when woman would no longer be considered the "gate of the devil." The revolt was directed not merely at evils in everyday life and at erroneous ideas which kept so many men from marrying, but also at the injustice of the punishment usually meted out to unmarried mothers, and at antiquated laws and customs. The revolt against existing laws will be considered first.

In a review of Lenz's "Zerbin" in the *Neue Bibliothek der schönen Wissenschaften und der freyen Künste* we read: "The story again prompts the sad reflection how so often human and divine justice are so utterly contradictory, because the former judges the external deed only, while the latter undoubtedly takes into consideration the whole series of causes which have involuntarily brought about the deed. Sometimes it is unavoidable, but in most cases the fault lies with the excessive severity of the laws, which in the end results in bribes given by those who can pay them, and does not lessen vice but instead leads to other crimes. Against such barbarity poets should direct their attacks, if they really want to be poets of the people. . . . Depict cruelties, abuses, vices and crimes, for the existence of which the prevailing religion, the severity or caprice and unnaturalness of many a law code is to blame."[39]

Pestalozzi, after discussing the circumstances which led a young woman to commit infanticide, concluded: "O you judges! The girl loved her babe, but because of your penal laws she killed it."[40] But the main attack against existing law was directed against its incompatibility with natural law. Justus Möser, who invariably defended current law and custom, in an essay "Ueber die zu unsern Zeiten verminderte

[39] Leipzig, 1778, XXII, 75ff.
[40] In "Ueber Gesetzgebung und Kindermord," p. 409. For similar opinions see Schlözer, *Stats-Anzeigen*, X, 352f.; *Idem*, V, 386; VII, 262f.

Schande der Huren und Hurkinder" classed every unmarried mother as a harlot and had absolutely no sympathy for
her or her child. He ridicules the "Philosophen" for defending the infanticide, and especially the unmarried mother who
did not kill her child. "The motives which have prompted
this defence have undoubtedly been great," he says, "nature, humanity and love of mankind have favored their
defence. But at bottom it is only the unpolitical philosophy
of our century which again shows its prowess. It is again the
new-fangled humanitarianism which is gaining at the expense
of patriotism. It is at most the Christian compassion which
fills a gap in our civil constitution, but which must not be
carried too far. The question cannot be simply: what are
the rights of mankind? when civil law is concerned. In the
natural state there is no marriage, and as soon as one transfers
conceptions of marriage from the civil state to the natural
state, there results a dangerous confusion the effects of which
are much more harmful than one imagines."[41] Möser denied
that there was any natural law which could be taken into
consideration in sexual matters, the only tangible source
being biblical tradition. That had been the contention of the
church for a thousand years; it had not yet relinquished its
control.

But Möser was mistaken. "The rights of nature have the
right of way above all others, and can not possibly be destroyed
by something which is merely a human convention," one of
the defenders of natural law aptly asserted. Hess insisted
that "civil laws may often be able to forbid what nature
permits, but they will fail in their attempt if they try to
abrogate the laws of nature: to command instinct, which is
essential to all creatures, to cease. I call that an attempt
to put nature in bondage."[42] Pestalozzi also asserted that
nature places on all humanity the necessity of satisfying the
sex impulse and that this necessity is accompanied by duties
of fatherhood and motherhood. "Custom and law sanctify
these duties in matrimony, but they are no less sacred with

[41] "Patriotische Phantasien." In "Sämmtliche Werke." Berlin, 1798,
II, 163f.

[42] "Freymüthige Gedanken," Hamburg, 1775, p. 58f.

unmarried parents, and a civil constitution which fails to recognize these is a fertile source of the abominations of immorality in Europe."[43] And Schlosser argued that the "power of the sexual desire and the power of fear know no law. . . . One need but look with one eye to know that your punishments for prostitution never have put a stop to the instinct of nature, and even if your punishments were made more lenient this instinct would not have any greater freedom."[44] This denial of the efficacy of the "Abschreckungs-theorie" was also made by List: "In the enjoyment of the present pleasure these girls are deaf, . . . the results of sexual irregularities seem to them of no consequence."[45]

What specific laws and customs did these writers have in mind? First of all capital punishment of infanticide. The whole controversy over this punishment went back to a little book by the Italian criminologist Beccaria referred to above.[46] That the subject was very popular is proved by Goethe's "Positiones juris." Number 53 reads: "Poenae capitales non abrogandae," and number 55: "An foemina partum re-center editum trucidans capite plectenda sit? quaestio est inter Doctores controversa."[47]

The most noted opponent of capital punishment in Germany was Viktor Barkhausen. In an article in the *Deutsches Museum*, entitled "Ueber Abschaffung der Todesstrafen," after discussing the injustice of capital punishment in general, he turns to the punishment of infanticide in particular. As to capital punishment in general, he accepts Beccaria's contention that it is neither necessary nor useful. "As for infanticide," he continues, "it presupposes a very extraordinary condition, in which the mind is so completely overwhelmed with notions of disgrace that neither virtue nor vice nor even death nor life itself nor any similar thing in this world is of any avail. The poor girl thinks only of disgrace and shame and honor and good name. Deprived of all human sympathy,

---

[43] "Ueber Gesetzgebung und Kindermord," p. 385.
[44] "Kleine Schriften," IV, p. 27.
[45] "Ueber Hurery und Kindermord," p. 1.
[46] *Supra*, p. 38.
[47] *Der junge Goethe*, ed. 2, II, 97.

not even in full possession of her senses, probably hardly
conscious of what she does, the mother hazards a deed which
alone seems to be able to save her from her dilemma—she
commits infanticide or even suicide.   Is it possible to imagine
that a girl under such circumstances would think of the death
penalty, that she would be horrified by the prospect of losing
her life, when she would only be too glad to give it if her honor
could be restored?"[48]   Sturz, Wekhrlin, Pestalozzi, Pfeil and
many others agreed with him, urging that capital punishment
should not be inflicted on infanticides.   It was also the opinion
of von Hess, Iselin, J. G. Schlosser, Klippstein, Thümmel and
a host of the contestants for the Mannheim prize.

Still others were not willing that this punishment should
be abolished, but agreed that the manner of execution should
be changed.   Pestalozzi called public executions "kalte
Gerechtigkeitsschauspiele."   He tells of a hysterical girl who
was so impressed by the solemnities attendant upon the
execution of an infanticide that she poisoned the child of her
master and found unusual delight in reporting it to the authorities and then in suffering the beautiful death by decapitation.
He cites this as an example how public executions were an in-
ducement to crime rather than a deterrent.

The argument in favor of the abolition of capital punishment met with stubborn resistance.   Nicolai and his staff on
the *Allgemeine Deutsche Bibliothek* consistently opposed every
suggestion to this end.   Möser wrote: "The question has
often been asked, Whence has the government the right to
punish this or that criminal by death?   It seems to me, we
should get much farther if we asked, Whence has the government the right to let this or that criminal live?"[49]   Kant too
opposed the abolition of this punishment but made two not-
able exceptions.   "There are two crimes," he said, "which
are worthy to be punished by death, but which are of such a
nature as to cast doubt on the right of legislation to decree
this penalty.   The cause of both crimes is the sense of honor
(Ehrgefühl).   In the one case it is the honor of sex (Geschlechts-

---

[48] *Deutsches Museum,* 1776², p. 676f.
[49] "Sämmtliche Werke," IV, 130.

ehre), in the other the honor of war (Kriegsehre). The
one crime is maternal infanticide, the other the duel. The
state requires absolute obedience to its demand that honor be
preserved; the unmarried mother tries to conform to this
demand by concealing her pregnancy and the birth of an illegitimate child, and then she kills it. To punish such a woman
is a contradiction to the requirement."[50]

Torture had been abolished in practically all parts of Europe,
at least in its more terrible forms. It is interesting to note
that Möser was willing to shift the power of decreeing torture
from the hands of the judges to a jury of twelve, as was cus-
tomary in England at that time.[51]

While there were many who recommended the abolition of
all manner of punishments for infanticide, most of the writers
still favored some form of punishment. Gottlieb Schlegel,
a contestant for the Mannheim prize, recommended an annual
sermon, to which all the infanticides in the local prison should
be brought. After the sermon they were to be led to the place
of execution and then back to prison. Schlosser suggested an
annual exhibition of infanticides for a period of six to ten years.
Klippstein proposed to differentiate the punishment of vicious
and of unfortunate infanticides. For the former he demanded
the death penalty invariably. "A week before the execution
the murderess shall be led through all the streets of the city.
There shall be solemnities of such a kind that all those who
see shall stand in awe with fear and trembling. The portrait
of the dead child would be carried ahead, also the instrument
of murder; the murderess would follow in a white gown be-
sprinkled with blood. She would be accompanied by a guard
and a procession of school children, the latter singing some
well chosen song of penance. The execution itself would take
place before the home of the guilty girl. In this way the horror of the crime would be deeply impressed on all minds".
For five years thereafter on the Sunday following the anniversary of the crime, a sermon would be preached from every
pulpit in the country on this terrible crime, and on the fol-

---

[50] "Sämmtliche Werke," Leipzig, 1868, VII, 153ff.
[51] "Sämmtliche Werke," V, 118f.

lowing day a well written essay on the same subject would be read in all the schools. The unfortunate infanticide would be condemned to life imprisonment. On the anniversary of her crime she, dressed in a special gown, a rope placed aronud her neck, and torches in her hands, would be led from the prison, taken to the church door, and the next day she would be exhibited in all the schools.[52]

The frequent proposal that the infanticide be punished annually prompts the question, Was this manner of punishment ever resorted to? We have at least one case to prove that it was. On the 31st of October, 1778, the king of Sweden decreed that no infanticide should be punished by death; instead she should be whipped and then imprisoned for life, or for a period of years. Every year, however, on the anniversary of the crime, she should be exposed publicly in a pillory for two hours or more and then be whipped, with stripes apportioned according to the circumstances under which the crime was committed.[53]

The revolt against existing canon law which dealt with sexual transgressions was no less vehement. Barkhausen lamented that so many law-makers and jurists were surrounded by a swarm of Roman Catholic and Protestant theologians. Hess accused the clergy of shirking their own responsibility. Instead of taking the sex problem in hand and eradicating the root of the trouble, they garrulously shifted the responsibility to the government by urging that it eradicate the sex evils even if many innocent people should perish. He points out that the fees charged for the performance of the wedding ceremony were exorbitant and unchristian, and "I know countries where the baptismal ceremony must be paid for doubly if the child was born out of wedlock. This is decidedly unjust, since the unmarried mother always has less means than a young married mother and because the father frequently cannot be found."[54]

The first specific object of attack was the old assertion that marriage had to be in accord with Mosaic law. Thümmel

[52] "Drei Preisschriften," p. 91f. Cf. also List, *loc. cit.*, p. 118f.
[53] Schlözer, *Briefwechsel*, V, 41f.
[54] "Freymüthige Gedanken," p. 58f.

would preach not of the grace of God, not of conversion, not of the trinity, but of human cruelty. He would do as the founder of the Christian church did, not search some old book of chronicles for the attitude of the people that lived a thousand years ago; he would take hold of the life of his day and stamp out the viper wherever it was found. Barkhausen asserted: "The laws of the Jews are not our laws and never were intended for us, for we are a people of a very different temperament, of a different character and of a different manner of thinking."

Then there was the bigotry of the church which Klinger so vehemently attacked in all of his literary productions. In his "Faust" he tells of a banquet in hell, at which the pages carry torches "made from the souls of monks, who . . . force the husband and father on his death bed to will his wealth to the church, without considering that their own adulterous brood must beg in the land."[55] Goethe too in the cathedral scene of "Faust" brings out very vividly the great gulf which had come into existence between Christ and the church. Coupland says of this scene: "In the cathedral scene the stern unbending sentence of the orthodox religious world, of the self-righteous saint. In the last scene of all the still small whisper from the High Throne, above the harshness of arrogant human virtue and ecclesiastical pride—the word of mercy and full pardon."[56] When Rühle once told Goethe that people called him a heathen he answered: "I a heathen? Well, I had Gretchen executed and I let Ottilie die of starvation; isn't that Christian enough? What more Christian act do they want?"[57]

I have pointed out in a preceding chapter that public church penance was abolished by Frederick the Great in 1746. In most of the states this example was followed soon thereafter, so that Kindleben could define church penance as an evil which had fallen into "disfavor and was gradually receiving the

[55] "Sämmtliche philosophische Romane," Leipzig, 1810, I, 33f. Cf. also Sprickmann, "Das Strumpfband," in *Deutsches Museum*, 1776[2], p. 1083f.

[56] William Chatterton Coupland, "The Spirit of Goethe's Faust." London, 1885, p. 174.

[57] See Gräf, "Goethe über seine Dichtungen," II, 2, 177.

consilium abeundi."[58]   Meissner expressed doubt as to whether infanticide would happen very often if church penance were abolished.[59]   Pfeil, who lived in Prussia, asserted that it was not to be denied that church penance, especially when administered by an unreasonable divine, often was the real cause of the commission of infanticide.[60]   But Möser again opposed this movement.   In an essay, "Also ist die Kirchen- busse so ganz nicht abzuschaffen," he says: "It should not be asserted on general grounds that an increase or decrease in the public disgrace of a fallen girl would have an influence on the commission of infanticide.   I personally feel sorry for the poor girl and I gladly believe that she has fallen in all inno- cence; but that is no reason for excusing her from undergoing church penance.   If the government wishes to do so, that is none of my business, but I shall not make any recommenda- tion to that effect."[61]

That Möser was mistaken in this opinion also is shown best by the petition which Goethe sent to Duke Karl August in 1780, requesting the Duke to abolish public church penance because, as he specifically stated, it was frequently the cause of infanticide.   Bernhard Suphan tries to trace the influence of Goethe's activity in this direction on two of his literary productions.   The one is a poem "Verantwortung eines Schwangern Mädgens," later entitled "Vor Gericht," the other the thirteenth chapter of the first book of "Wilhelm Meisters Lehrjahre."   The poem however probably dates back to the Strassburg period and the passage in "Wilhelm Meisters Lehrjahre" at least to 1776.   It would be better therefore not to limit the revelation of Goethe's interest in unmarried motherhood in these two literary productions to his attempts to have public church penance abolished in 1780, but rather to take them as two more instances of the intensity of the poet's sympathy for the unmarried mother.   Beginning with the *positiones juris* at Strassburg this sympathy was revealed more

---

[58] "Studenten-Lexicon," p. 48.

[59] Carl Friedrich Meissner, "Zwo Abhandlungen über die Frage: Sind die Findel-Häuser vorteilhaft oder schädlich?"   Göttingen, 1779, p. 105.

[60] "Drei Preisschriften," p. 29.

[61] "Patriotische Phantasien."   Berlin, 1843, V, 107f.; *loc. cit.*, 110f.

and more in "Werther," "Stella" and the "Urfaust," and the intensity of the appeal in the poem and in "Wilhelm Meister" referred to above indicates that this sympathy had not abated in the least. In all of these productions the poet extends his sympathy by taking an active part in the girl's defense.[62] In the poem the girl refuses to tell the name of the father of her illegitimate child.

> Soll Spott und Hohn getragen sein,
> Trag' ich allein den Hohn.
> Ich kenn' ihn wohl, er kennt mich wohl,
> Und Gott weiss auch davon.
>
> Herr Pfarrer und Herr Amtmann ihr,
> Ich bitte, lasst mich in Ruh!
> Es ist mein Kind, es bleibt mein Kind,
> Ihr gebt mir ja nichts dazu.

In spite of her unfortunate condition, the girl is truly a mother, only the harshness of the representatives of church and state could force her to kill her child. The "Eternal Feminine" which Goethe depicted so wonderfully, is here also revealed in the girl's refusal to cause her lover any inconvenience. She is willing to bear the burden alone.

In a "Herderisches Votum" of 1780 Herder tells in forceful prose the intensity of his sympathy for the unmarried mother. "Da steht eine arme Weibsperson, die vielleicht der Augenblick berückt hat, die durch ihren kurzen Fehltritt Glück, Ehre, Gut, vielleicht auf Zeitlebens eingebüsst hat; sie kniet weinend nieder und wird ein Schauspiel des Diebes, des kalten Frevlers und Bösewichts, der bei ihr steht. . . . Als Pfarrer soll ich die arme Knieende mit grossem Pomp fragen: Glaubst du wahrhaftig, dass ich als ordentlicher Pfarrer dieses Orts von Gottes wegen Macht und Gewalt habe, dir diese öffentliche Sünde zu vergeben? und sie kann mich fragen: Glaubst du aber auch, dass du als ein ordentlicher Pfarrer dieses Ortes von Gottes wegen *nicht* Macht und Gewalt hast, meiner

---

[62] See "Goethe im Conseil. Urkundliches aus seiner amtlichen Thätigkeit 1778-1785," in vol. VI, 597ff. of *Vierteljahrschrift für Litteraturgeschichte.* Weimar, 1893.

Nachbarin, die die Ehe gebrochen, meinem Nachbar, dem Hofdiener, dem Soldaten, dem Diebe, dem Verächter der Sakramente, Sünde zu vergeben oder zu behalten?'' Goethe and Herder very clearly realized that of all those who commit sins, the unmarried mother was punished most severely in comparison with the gravity of her crime.

The nuns also come in for their share of sympathy as sacrifices to arbitrary power. The poets of the period want them set free, so that they can be human, and do their human duty as mothers of families. So the nun who cannot forget that she was a woman before she was a nun finds special favor. The abbess in Leisewitz' ''Julius von Tarent'' is asked by Julius: ''What separated you from the world, devotion or these walls? Have you never loved? What were you first, nun or woman?'' To which she answers: ''O Prince, let me alone. Nineteen years I have wept and still there are tears. . . . O my Ricardo!''[63]

There were three types of girls who were sent to convents against their will. First, there were those whose parents were unable or unwilling to pay the large wedding-fees. Secondly, there were those put into convents for safety. The third class consisted of those sent to the convents because of some undue influence, the real object being to obtain the property which the girls would inherit. The latter happened particularly if there was only one girl in the family, or if she was the only child. Johann Martin Miller and Anton Matthias Sprickmann wrote so much of nuns that they were called ''Nonnendichter.''[64]

A suggestion often met with in the writings of the period is to punish the seducer. Because of his superior knowledge

[63] Cf. Goethe, ''Gottfried von Berlichingen,'' Act I, Maria to Weislingen: ''Sie [die Äbtissin meines Klosters] hatte geliebt, usw.'' See *Der junge Goethe,* Ed. 2, III, 198.

[64] For a discussion of ''Nonnenpoesie'' see Heinrich Kraeger, ''Johann Martin Millers Gedichte.'' Bremen, 1892. Cf. Miller's ''Siegwart. Eine Klostergeschichte.'' Stuttgart, 1844, II, p. 95; Stelzer, ''Christinchen'' (1780) in *Taschenbuch für Dichter und Dichterfreunde,* XI, 86f.; Thümmel, ''Der heilige Kilian.'' Herausgegeben von F. F. Hempel. Leipzig, 1818; Sprickmann, ''Das Neujahrsgeschenk, Eine Klosteranekdote,'' in *Deutsches Museum,* 1776², p. 788f; etc.

of the laws and by means of perjury the seducer was generally able to escape punishment. One contributor to Schlözer's *Briefwechsel* complains that there are so many who say "Beccaria this, and Beccaria that, but no one recommends that the seducer be punished severely, very severely."[65] Another says: "Punish the instigator of the whole trouble, who seduces innocence and dishonors virtue, for whoever wishes to eradicate an evil must begin at the very source."[66] Hess ironically suggested that a "fiery youth whose whole nervous system becomes so tense when he sees a beautiful girl that even Socrates under similar conditions would have been compelled to struggle with a wavering conscience—such a youth shall, if he cannot pay a fine, be publicly flogged because he has yielded to his temperament."[67] Others, and there were not a few, wanted to force the seducer to marry the girl.[68] Still others insisted that he must support the unmarried mother and his illegitimate child. This was to be done directly or indirectly through taxation.[69] One frequently meets with the suggestion that all bachelors should be taxed, the proceeds of the tax to go to the support of institutions which were to care for the unmarried mother and her child. This could be an income tax, or the bachelor's estate would automatically go to the state upon his death. Hippel, himself a bachelor for life, recommended that from one tenth to one sixth of the estate of every bachelor be turned over to asylums for the poor.[70]

Nicolai and his staff vehemently opposed the suggestion that the seducer be forced to marry the unfortunate girl, for "such marriages would always be unhappy and it would therefore be a medicine which would be worse than the disease."[71]

Erich Schmidt in his "Heinrich Leopold Wagner, Goethes

---

[65] XI, 470.

[66] *Idem*, X, 354.

[67] "Freymüthige Gedanken," p. 61.

[68] *Allgemeine Deutsche Bibliothek*, 62, 70; *idem*, 113, 55f.; "Drei Preisschriften," p. 86.; etc.

[69] "Drei Preisschriften," p. 149; List, *loc. cit.*, p. 50; Hermes, "Sophiens Reise," p. 619; etc.

[70] "Sämmtliche Werke," V, 27f.

[71] *Allgemeine Deutsche Bibliothek*, 113, 55f.; 62, 70f.

Jugendgenosse" pointed out that the establishment of foundling houses was equally favored and opposed.[72] The most
elaborate discussion of the subject is by Carl Friedrich Meissner in two essays entitled "Zwo Abhandlungen über die
Frage: Sind die Findel-Häuser vorteilhaft oder schädlich?"[73]
Meissner was decidedly opposed to their establishment. He
gives a brief history of foundling-houses in Greece and Italy,
and later of those in Paris and London, to show how miserably
they had failed. He then gives several reasons why he is
opposed to them. First, they are very expensive, second, they
fail in the object of their establishment, namely the salvation
of poor children, and third, they cause great harm in that they
increase and encourage illegitimacy. He argues that foundling-houses really do increase illegitimacy and that the mortality of the foundlings is so high that the houses may be
called "Mördergruben." Pfeil, in his prize essay, asserted
that nine-tenths of the children put into these institutions
died in infancy.[74] A contributor to Schlözer's *Briefwechsel*
reported that in Cassel, of the thirty-six children received in
the local foundling-house, thirty-two died.[75] Schlözer asserted
that he knew many men who were well able to marry, "but
they keep concubines (Menscher) and as soon as one of these
gives birth to a child it is taken to a foundling-house, where in
a few weeks it dies." That the foundling-house is an insufficient means to stop unmarried motherhood, or infanticide,
is a stereotyped assertion of the period.[76] Pastor Dürr in
a report to the *Göttingen Gelehrten Anzeigen* claimed that
the "mortality of children has greatly increased in the last
twenty years and with it the number of illegitimate children."[77]

Hess, however, was in favor of these institutions.[78] So too

[72] See page 92f.

[73] Göttingen, 1779.

[74] "Drei Preisschriften," p. 31f.

[75] VIII, 44.

[76] See *Allgemeine Deutsche Bibliothek*, 54, 111; *idem*, 54, 113; *idem*, 88, 91f.;
idem, 113, 55f.; Pestalozzi in his essay, p. 381f.; Johann Peter Süssmilch, "Die
göttliche Ordnung." Berlin, 1765, part 1, p. 193; Klippstein in the prize
essay, p. 89; Kreuzfeld, p. 121f., etc.

[77] "Zwo Abhandlungen," p. 74.

[78] "Freymüthige Gedanken," p. 38f.

Iselin and J. G. Schlosser.[79]   But they belonged to the minority.

All these manifold suggestions for the amelioration or eradication of evils were consistently opposed by Möser at every step of the agitation. "I am not so sure," he says on one occasion, "that the government is in duty bound to seek out the causes of crimes in order to prevent their repetition. According to my opinion the government must always look upon the consequence of crime and let the rest alone. Even if hundreds of criminals should commit suicide in prison to evade the wheel or the gallows, that would be no reason for the government to let a single criminal go unpunished. What would happen if a general, in order to prevent desertion, should excuse even the smallest causes which lead to this action? He must punish everything with equal severity—the perjury of which a soldier is guilty when he deserts the army, and the soldier who sleeps at his post, even if the cause was the excessive heat of the preceding day."[80]

[79] Iselin in an essay "Ueber den Kindermord," in part 4 of *Ephemeriden der Menschheit*, 1778.   Schlosser in "Kleine Schriften," IV, 53.
[80] "Patriotische Phantasien," V, 109f.

CHAPTER III

"The end and aim of all literature," said Matthew Arnold,
"if one considers it attentively, is, in truth, nothing but a
criticism of life. . . . The action of two distinct factors can
be traced in any work of creative literature, the personality
of the author, and the mental atmosphere of the age." Alfred
Freiherr von Berger says that "the subjects of the drama are
typical human experiences. . . . I could point out this characteristic of genuinely dramatic material in numberless
literary productions. In every man there is a piece of Othello,
every woman has looked at her husband through Desdemona
eyes, in every marriage there occur Othello scenes, tempered
and modified of course, every man who is an 'aimless, restless
monster,' like Faust, has enjoyed the fragrance of maiden-
hood's flower, and then has deceived the hope he has awakened.
It is not necessary that there should be seduction, infanticide
or even death, but no one can deny that he has experienced
some part of the Faust-Gretchen tragedy in one way or another."[1]

The universality of the tragedy of unmarried motherhood
has always justified its poetic treatment. But the per-
meation of the mental atmosphere of the last three decades of
the eighteenth century with sympathy for the unfortunate
girl who was compelled by circumstances to get rid of her
child, explains the extensive use of the theme in the imaginative literature of the time. It is important to note that too
much emphasis has been placed by critics on the individual
experience of writers as being the sole source for the inspiration
of their literary productions. Undoubtedly Bürger's experiences with the Leonhard girls played a part in the production
of "Des Pfarrers Tochter von Taubenhain," while Sprick-

[1] "Dramaturgische Vorträge." Wien, 1891, pp. 35, 38.

mann's affair with a certain lady for whom Bürger suggested a place of refuge in part inspired him to write his poems and dramatic sketches. One can imagine that Maler Müller's desertion of Charlotte Kärner influenced his ballad "Das braune Fräulein" and his idyls "Das Nusskernen" and "Die Schaafschur," just as Wagner's "Die Kindermörderinn," Lenz's dramas "Die Soldaten" and "Der Hofmeister," as well as his novelette "Zerbin," may have been influenced by the experience of the elder von Kleist, whom Lenz tutored, with a girl in Strassburg. Friederike Brion undoubtedly gave Goethe the inspiration for the theme of the deserted girl in "Clavigo," "Götz," "Stella" and above all in "Faust." But even in these cases one cannot say that the personal experience of the writers furnished the sole source of the literary production. The preacher's daughter in Bürger's poem cannot be identified with either of the Leonhard girls. Bürger's interest in the theme of infanticide dates back to 1772, when he worked out an abstract of a case of infanticide.[2] The deserted girl and the infanticide in Müller's productions is not Charlotte Kärner. Ida in Sprickmann's poem is not the court-lady, neither Gustchen, Marie nor Evchen can be said to be the deserted sweetheart of the elder von Kleist, Gretchen in "Faust" certainly is not Friederike. And then how should we account for the productions of Schiller, Hippel, Hermes, A. G. Meissner, Gemmingen and others, to whose personal experience we can trace no definite relationship with any specific case of unmarried motherhood?

An analysis of the literature of the period will prove that the great predilection for the theme is for the most part a reflex of the revolt discussed in the preceding chapter. And one of the most striking characteristics of the literature is its didacticism. Indeed the revolt inherently contained this element. We have seen how the theory which sought to prevent crimes by terrible punishments was displaced by a new theory which taught that crimes are best prevented by seeking out and eliminating their causes. In one respect, at least, both theories agreed, in that both sought to prevent.

<hr>

[2] See Karl Goedeke: "Bürger in Göttingen und Gelliehausen," p. 92.

The difference in the theories lies in the method of prevention. On the old theory, girls were warned by letting them see what terrible penalties were imposed for unmarried motherhood, on the new theory, by showing in detail how the tragedy of infanticide developed and ended.

English writers led the way in this attempt to warn prospective criminals. George Lillo and Edward Moore did but illustrate the "Abschreckungstheorie." Barnwell in the former's "George Barnwell" is perverted by Millwood from a virtuous youth into a thief and murderer. In the last scene the "crushed" public sees the gallows on the stage and the young moralist Trueman warns:

> With bleeding hearts and weeping eyes we show
> A humane gen'rous sense of others' woe;
> Unless we mark what drew their ruin on,
> And by avoiding that prevent our own.

Moore too, in "The Gamester," moralizes: "let frailer minds take warning."

The Germans, who for centuries had been good imitators, followed the example of their English cousins. Wagner uses the civil law book at the end of "Die Kindermörderinn" with no other purpose than to warn prospective unmarried mothers of the inexorableness of the law. That too is the object of the warning in Matthias Claudius' "Schönheit und Unschuld. Ein Sermon an die Mädchen." After discussing the virtues of the fair sex and how they are usually lost, the writer exclaims: "Flee the man who makes you believe that chastity and virtue are nonsense and superstition! Even if he were dressed in gold and pearls he is a rascal, a poisonous rattlesnake."[3] Blumauer's poem "Lehren an ein Mädchen" contains a similar warning.

> Drum hüte dich vor dieser Pest,
> Und so ein Mann sich finden lässt,
> Der dein begehrt, so sehe nicht
> Dem Freyer blos nur in's Gesicht:

[3] "Sämmtliche Werke des Wandsbecker Boten." Gotha, 1882, I, 275ff.

> Denn wiss, dass oft ein böser Mann
> In Engelslarve stecken kann.[4]

Bürger in "Hummel-Lied" compares maidens to flowers and boys to bumble bees and then warns

> Ihr Mägdlein mögt euch hüten![5]

Maler Müller devotes the first six stanzas of "Das braune Fräulein" to warning girls, lest they meet with the fate of the brown maiden. The fourth stanza reads

> Es beb' dein junges Herzchen
> Verborgen jeder List;
> Dein junges fühlend Herzchen
> Das ganz nur Unschuld ist.[6]

Frequently the warning is placed at the end of the poem to serve as a sort of moral. Fr. Schmit attributes the fall of Molly in "Bey Molly's Grab" to her innocence and inexperience with the ways of the world. The poem concludes

> Kein Mädchen seh mit stolzem Richterblicke
> Auf die Gefallene herab!
> Mit Zittern denkt an die Gefahren, die euch drohn,
> Und weint bey ihrem frühen Grab.[7]

The most frightful example of the motif of warning in the fiction of the period is Thümmel's story, in "Die Reise in die mittäglichen Provinzen von Frankreich," of a girl whose ugliness was made beautiful by substituting for her own hair and teeth those of an infanticide, whose body after her execution came into the hands of her guardian, a physician. Thümmel says: "The girl only lacked beautiful hair and good teeth to change her entire appearance. He [the physician] accordingly took the dark hair and the white teeth of the decapitated infanticide and decorated his foster daughter with the brown locks which so picturesquely roll down her white neck, and

---

[4] "Aloys Blumauer's sämmtliche Werke." Königsberg, 1827, II, 73ff.
[5] "Sämmtliche Werke," Göttingen, 1829, II, 160f.
[6] See "Stürmer und Dränger." Hrsg. von A. Sauer, III, 266ff.
[7] *Taschenbuch für Dichter und Dichterfreunde*, II, 61ff.

substituted for the black pegs in her mouth teeth of pure pearl. Did he do the girl an injustice? . . . No, he not only made the girl more beautiful than she was before, but he guaranteed her virtue. . . . What warning could protect an innocent girl more effectively against the first false step than the heritage of one who had fallen so low?"[8]

Didacticism is no less common in the dramas of the period. Erich Schmidt would be quite right in condemning the use of so much crass realism were it not for the conscious attempt to apply the "Abschreckungstheorie." That it was conscious is proved by Wagner's defense of the first version of "Die Kindermörderinn" when he published the revised version under the title "Evchen Humbrecht, oder, Ihr Mütter hütet Euch." "To awaken vile thoughts is only permitted if one wishes to use means to make vice hateful and abominable," Wagner asserted. Klinger also found it necessary to defend his rather free use of vulgarity. While his drama "Das leidende Weib" has nothing directly to do with our subject, his remarks indicate why he used so much crass realism in his "Fausts Leben, Thaten und Höllenfahrt," realism which is so gross at times that it is unreadable. "I wanted to depict the value of virtue by example and action," he says, "I wanted to make the reader feel it and to teach how remorse and punishment avenge its loss."[9]

Bürger too was possessed of the same idea of warning or frightening. In a letter dated November 13, 1773, to Boie he tells of a drama which he is going to write: "I am brooding over a mighty production, which is nothing less than a tragedy from civil life. The plan is made, my own invention, and a few scenes have been written down—scenes which will make your hair stand on end."[10] And Sprickmann plans a drama in which the parents of an illegitimate child meet their doom

[8] "Sämmtliche Werke." Leipzig, 1839, VI, 95ff.

[9] For Wagner's whole defense see Erich Schmidt, "Heinrich Leopold Wagner," p. 97. For Klinger's defense see Max Rieger, "Klinger in der Sturm und Drangperiode." Darmstadt, 1880, I, 377f.

[10] That the poet had a drama on infanticide in mind in the quotation given here is proved by his assertion to Boie when the latter referred to Wagner's "Die Kindermörderinn": "Der Titel frappirt mich, weil ich ein dramatisches Süjet unter eben dem Titel lang im Busen herumgetragen habe." As far as we know, Bürger never thought of writing a drama on any other subject.

in the last scene, the mother and father committing suicide, while the innocent child sends the terrified audience home by its incessant crying when the curtain falls.[11]

The theme of the unmarried mother lends itself readily to realistic detail and the placing of particular emphasis on these elements explains largely why so much of the literature on the unmarried mother, written at this time, did not live. Practically all of the writers were able by their writings to win sympathy for the unmarried mother. They thus fulfilled the first requirement of tragedy, to excite pity. But in the fulfillment of the second requirement, the instillation of fear, most of them failed utterly. They failed to distinguish between horror and fear. Or perhaps it were better to say that they did not wish to distinguish between the two. I am inclined to believe the writers of the period wished to arouse extreme horror as well as utter disgust for those things which led up to infanticide. That explains the portrayal of seduction and infanticide itself, as well as the immediate circumstances surrounding them, with the most minute detail.

Bürger particularly delighted in detailed description of the immediate circumstances attendant on seduction, and consciously or unconsciously he put into this description an element of didacticism. In "Des Pfarrers Tochter von Taubenhain" he describes the seduction of Rosette by the young squire of Falkenstein.

> Er zog sie zur Laube, so düster und still,
> Von blühenden Bohnen umdüftet.
> Da pocht' ihr das Herzchen, da schwoll ihr die Brust;
> Da wurde vom glühenden Hauche der Lust
> Die Unschuld zu Tode vergiftet. . . .
>
> Bald, als auf duftendem Bohnenbeet
> Die röthlichen Blumen verblühten,
> Da wurde dem Mädchen so übel und weh;
> * * * * * * * *
> Da wurde dem Mädchen das Brüstchen zu voll,
> Das seidene Röckchen zu enge.[12]

[11] See A. Sauer in introduction to "Stürmer und Dränger," I, 46.

[12] "Sämmtliche Werke," II, 32f. Cf. also his poem "Der wohlgesinnte Liebhaber," *idem*, II, 214f.

Wagner in "Die Kindermörderinn" goes so far as to put rape on the stage. Gröningseck, after putting the mother of Evchen to sleep by means of a potion, tries to embrace the girl. She resists and flees into the adjoining room, shrieking: "Mother! Mother! I am lost." Gröningseck pursues her, closes the door behind him, and the noise in the room lets the spectator guess the rest. A few minutes later Evchen dashes from the room with the announcement: "Mother! unnatural mother! sleep, . . . sleep forever! . . . for your daughter has been made a harlot."[13]

It must not be assumed, however, that all the poets of the period of Storm and Stress portrayed seduction with such realistic detail. Goethe and Schiller in dealing with this theme proved themselves better artists. Instead of detailed description of seduction and the circumstances preceding and following it, they merely allude to it. Luise in Schiller's "Die Kindesmörderin" says

> Weh! vom Arm des falschen Manns umwunden
> Schlief Luisens Tugend ein.[14]

In Goethe's "Faust" Gretchen, after a happy tryst with Faust, tells him she would gladly leave the door unbolted if her mother slept more soundly.[15] Faust gives her the sleeping-potion and then departs. In the scene "Am Brunnen" we discover indirectly that the seduction has taken place and

[13] Act I. Erich Schmidt asserted that this act was absolutely impossible on the stage. A. Sauer and others agreed with him. Karl Freye in the introduction to "Sturm und Drang," I, lv, denied this impossibility.

[14] "Schiller's Sämtliche Werke." Säkular Ausgabe, I, 30ff.

[15] Critics have questioned Gretchen's innocence in giving Faust permission to come to her room before marriage. But it is worth remembering that there still existed in different parts of Germany, when Goethe wrote his drama, a widely sanctioned custom, the survival of a sort of trial marriage called "Probenacht." According to this custom, which only existed among the lower classes, girls regularly accorded to their favored wooer the privileges of a husband. If conception resulted and the lover was honorable, legal marriage followed. The danger of the custom lay in the lover's being of a frivolous or vicious mind and his refusal to accept the social consequences of his paternity. Faust proved to be a lover of the latter type—hence the tragedy of Gretchen. A lengthy discussion of the custom is F. C. J. Fischer's "Ueber die Probenächte der teutschen Bauernmädchen," Berlin, 1780. The essay is reprinted in J. Scheible, "Das Schaltjahr," Stuttgart, 1846, II, 681ff., III, 266ff., 438ff.

that Gretchen is a prospective mother. The poet lets Bärbelchen tell of the fall of a playmate and Gretchen's simple

Und bin nun selbst der Sünde bloss!

tells the whole story.

While Bürger liked to portray the crass realism in seduction,
Sprickmann had a predilection for the horrors attendant upon
the commission of infanticide. His first poem on infanticide
"Ida" is the best example. Humfried, who has seduced Ida,
deserts her for another girl, Luitberga. In a forest cavern
the unfortunate girl gives birth to her illegitimate child.
While she is cursing her fate, Humfried is driven, by his conscience, out into the night to find peace. On this sojourn he
sees a light in the distance, and going to the place whence it
comes, he finds Ida and the child on the straw. For a moment
all is silent and then Ida breaks out in her fury:

> "Herzliebster, wo bist du?
> Sieh! bist ja nun Vater!—Wo bist du?
> Da nimm es, nimm's Bübchen in Armen!
> Sieh, 's will dich lieben! so habe doch Erbarmen!
> *   *   *   *   *   *   *   *
>
> Da, nimm's! 's will lieben dich ja!
> Da Humfried!—Hölle!—Humfried's du!
> Und habe dich im Schoos?—Zum Teufel!—Hu!—Hu!—"
> O Himmel! Mit wütender Macht
> Geschleudert am Felsen, zerkracht—
> Des armen Kindes zart Gebein.
> *   *   *   *   *   *   *   *
>
> Dess erwacht die Mutter aus ihrer Wut,
> Fällt hin über's Kind, und leckt von der Stirne
> Ihm Blut und Gehirne,
> Und rauft sich das Haar und schlägt sich das Blut
> Mit rasender Faust aus den Brüsten.[16]

Wagner even put infanticide on the stage. In the last act

[16] *Deutsches Museum*, 1777[1], p. 120ff. Sprickmann must have delighted in
portraying such scenes for we find one similar to the above in his dramatic
sketch "Horry" in *Deutsches Museum*, 1778[1], p. 5f. Cf. also A. G. Meissner,
"Die Mörderin" in *Deutsches Museum*, 1779[1], 379ff.; Lenz's "Zerbin" in the
same magazine, 1776[1], 193f.; etc.

of "Die Kindermörderinn" Evchen takes a hair needle
and stabs her child in the temple. In order not to hear the
screaming of the child she sings

> Eya Pupeya!
> Schlaf Kindlein! schlaf wohl!
> Schlaf ewig wohl!
> Ha ha ha, ha ha!

When the child is dead she kisses away the blood from its
temple while she soliloquizes: "What is that?—sweet! very
sweet! but afterwards bitter—ha, now I recognize it—blood
of my own child!"

In the best dramatic literature one fails to find a single
production in which infanticide is put on the stage. One
recalls that Horace objected to Medea killing her children on
the stage in the presence of the spectators. The explanation
for this aversion to seeing infanticide on the stage is found in
the aversion which society has for the crime in real life. The
commission of the act by the mother is contrary to natural
law. From a purely artistic standpoint an allusion to the
act is quite enough to set the imagination to work and so
produces the fear required by tragedy. The poem by Schiller
lets Luise recall the vows of Joseph. This excites hatred for
her unfaithful lover, and Luise tells how the feeling affected
her:

> Seine Eide donnern aus dem Grabe wieder,
> Ewig, ewig würgt sein Meineid fort,
> Ewig—hier umstrickte mich die Hyder—
> Und vollendet war der Mord.

Influenced by Meissner and Sprickmann, Schiller then goes
on to give a more minute description of the infanticide proper
and what followed it.

> Seht! da lag's entseelt zu meinen Füssen—
> Kalt hinstarrend, mit verworrnem Sinn
> Sah ich seines Blutes Ströme fliessen,
> Und mein Leben floss mit ihm dahin—.

Gemmingen in "Der deutsche Hausvater," which was

popular on the German stage for twenty-five years,[17] resorts
to a clever device to temper the terribleness of infanticide.
In the first act he has Lotte write to Karl: "If Karl should
desert me, then, terrible as it is, I would with my own hands
murder the child, which I shall have by him, and that would
be maternal kindness; then I would let them execute me publicly." Later in the fourth act Karl comes to take leave of
Lotte. His mission, which is difficult enough in itself, is only
made more difficult by the artist, who suddenly broaches the
suitability of infanticide for plastic art. He says: "The
artists of antiquity knew how to appeal to their nation so
effectively: I think we could do that too if we depicted subjects which concern each one particularly. For instance,
there is a most terrible thing, infanticide. According to my
feeling, I know of nothing more terrible in all nature." Then
by way of emphasizing his thought the artist produces a series
of sketches of the successive steps in the career of an unmarried
mother who is driven by force of circumstances to kill her
child. On the first sketcht here is "an unfortunate girl who has
just killed her child." "Notice the despair expressed by that
one line. Do you feel that, Count?" he asks Karl. The latter
answers: "Yes, inexpressibly." He saw in the picture all
the tragic possibilities for Lottchen, whom he had got with
child and of whom he had come to take leave forever. The
artist proceeds: "And this second sketch. There she lies
now, the mother, the very picture of misfortune, the dead
child pressed to her bosom. She doesn't want to leave it after
all. And here the guard, who is about to take her to court,
and there the poor old father, who in despair is going to. . . ."
At this point Lotte faints and the conversation is interrupted.
By bringing in the sketches Gemmingen divides the interest
of the reader. If he had simply let the artist tell of the tragic
possibilities of Lotte's condition his description of the infanticide would have called forth disgust and horror only. As it
is, he appeals to the emotion of fear and intensifies our pity for
the naïve girl. A reviewer in the *Litteratur und Theater
Zeitung* records the fact that this method of treating the theme

[17] *Euphorion*, XIII, 791.

was very effective on the stage. The reviewer after discussing the merits of the drama in general, states that this scene was one of two which always gained the greatest applause.[18]

Goethe, too, the greatest literary artist of the time, veils the horrible details. Gretchen is in prison before we know that she has killed her child. The modern reader who does not know of the laws in regard to the unmarried mother of that time would be justified in asking: Why is Gretchen in prison? Is it because she virtually murdered her mother? No, there is nothing to indicate that she was arrested and later condemned to die because of this crime. She was arrested because she was an unmarried mother. Even if she had not murdered her child she would have suffered the penalty of death, for the law inflicted that equally for concealment of pregnancy, concealment of child-birth and infanticide. Any one of these three would have been sufficient to convict her. The reader of "Faust" knows long before Gretchen is in prison that she is trying to hide her condition, he therefore knows too that when she is found out she will be placed in prison. It was easy for Goethe's contemporaries to understand why she was in prison even before they learned that she had killed her child. The girl's crime is her state of unmarried motherhood and the *consequent* infanticide, not merely the killing of the child.

This explains why Gretchen only mentions the killing of her child as one of a whole series of acts which led up to her arrest and conviction. In her ravings she reviews these deeds. There were the happy days of love-making, the sleep-potion for the mother, the contempt of the world and the church, the death of Valentine and the murder of her child. And when she comes to the latter there is no minute description, there is only a direction to Faust to go and rescue the poor babe.

> Geschwind! Geschwind!
> Rette dein armes Kind.
> Fort! Immer den Weg

[18] See Cäsar Flaischlen, "Otto Heinrich Freiherr von Gemmingen. Mit einer Vorstudie über Diderot als Dramatiker." Stuttgart, 1890, p. 104f.

Am Bach hinauf,
Über den Steg
In den Wald hinein,
Links, wo die Planke steht,
Im Teich.
Fass es nur gleich!
Es will sich heben
Es zappelt noch!
Rette! rette!

The imagination is set to work and when she has told Faust
of the fate of their child she hurries on and the reader fears
for her end.

The revolt against the methods of punishing the unmarried
mother who killed her child was preceded by a differentiation
between the harlot and the girl who became an infanticide by
force of circumstances. And the sympathy of this period
was lavished only on the unmarried mother of the latter type.
It was believed that some girls intentionally practiced prostitution without being compelled to do so. Some writers even
refused to concede that girls became mothers unmarried
involuntarily. Runde, an ardent defender of capital punishment, believed that every infanticide was really a vicious
harlot. He asserted that in no case did human nature sink
to so low a level as in the commission of this deed.[19] Of
course no writer went so far as to justify the act. Pfeil for
instance, one of the ardent defenders of the unmarried mother,
calls infanticide the most unnatural, the most despicable of all
crimes.[20] Schummel in "Empfindsame Reisen durch Deutschland," in one of the episodes, tells of a visit to the execution
of a child-murderess and leaves a whole page blank as an
appropriate proof of incapacity to express his emotions.
Herder in "Ideen zur Philosophie der Geschichte der Menschheit" tells of the fathers of antiquity who were driven by
need and hunger to kill their own children. Even to them the
crime was so horrible and they so disliked to commit it that
they consecrated the children to death even while they were

[19] *Deutsches Museum,* 1777[1], 329f.
[20] "Drei Preisschriften," p. 11.

unborn, before hearing their voice. "Many an infanticide," Herder continues, "confessed that nothing was so hard for her and nothing remained so vivid in her memory as the first pitiful cry, the imploring voice of the child."[21]

List in his contest essay enumerates twelve types of girls who became infanticides, and only one is the harlot. All the others were at first girls of good character. Very frequently the father or mother of the girl was dead. The preacher's daughter, as we find her in Bürger's "Des Pfarrers Tochter von Taubenhain," or in Maler Müller's "Das Nusskernen," the artist's daughter, as in Gemmingen's "Der deutsche Hausvater," the peasant's daughter, as in Hölty's "Adelstan und Röschen," or the daughter of other honest and respectable parents are the typical girls who found it necessary to commit infanticide. Maler Müller tells of a widow who had a quiet, honest, industrious daughter who became an unmarried mother; Jung-Stilling of another girl who was good and virtuous, who had no desire to lead an immoral life, who had a tender heart, was beautiful and pious. Pestalozzi devotes a whole section of his essay "Ueber Gesetzgebung und Kindermord" to the girl who became the victim of seduction on going into service in the city; Gretchen in Goethe's "Faust" is a poor but virtuous girl, her father is dead and she has been denied the ordinary pleasures of youth. Her first experience of love is with a man of the world, who is ruled solely by passion.

The real tragic interest lies in the contrast between the loveliness of motherhood and the awfulness of child-murder. Bettina in Buchholz' sketch by the same name has lived her life as if in a light morning dream, playing like a child and always the happiest of her playmates. She would sit at the spinning wheel, while she sang songs of the birds and trees to her baby brother in the cradle at her side. Later she was seduced by a stranger while she was working in the city, and still later in order to rid herself of the unbearable burden, killed her own child. Gretchen in "Faust" is "the most child-like, good-hearted and the most naïve of all of Goethe's woman characters. She becomes the murderess of her own

---

[21] "Herders Ausgewählte Werke." Stuttgart und Berlin, I, 131.

child, which she has received from the man she loved most in all the world." Sympathy for her is increased by the fact that, as if by foreboding, she has performed the burdensome duties of motherhood for her baby sister.

What were the motives which conspired to drive the unmarried mother to become a murderess? One of the motifs used by nearly all writers of the period—and its source was real life—was the desertion of her who was soon to be an unmarried mother by the man who saw no sanctity in the sex relation and was averse to marriage. The forsaken unmarried mother, indeed, most frequently became the infanticide.

Karl, in Gemmingen's drama, says to Sophie, his sister: "Tell me, wouldn't it be inhuman to desert the girl without saying anything, the girl who has already dreamed that she would be my wife, and who will soon be a mother?" Sprickmann in his dramatic sketch "Horry" depicts Horry as almost mad with despair, going to a cemetery, where he intends to put an end to his miserable existence. Just as he reaches the place a funeral procession arrives. It is the funeral of one of his victims. He sits by on a tomb-stone while the burial ceremony is performed. After everybody is gone, he goes to the grave and attempts to dig up the remains that have just been interred. In the midst of his work a spirit appears, which says: "I am Marie, the beloved, the forsaken one." A little later a second spirit, and then a third appears each wailing its pathetic: "I am the beloved, the forsaken one." That in at least two cases infanticide was committed is recorded a little later in the same scene.

Ida in Sprickmann's poem by the same title and Marie in his "Mariens Reden bei ihrer Trauung" are also forsaken girls who are driven to mad deeds. In the one case the girl commits infanticide and then suicide, in the other suicide after she has forced her lover, who has forsaken her for another, to marry her. Läuffer in Lenz's "Der Hofmeister" and Desportes in his "Die Soldaten" both run away and leave the pregnant girls to their fate. Marie in Lenz's "Zerbin," Rosette in Bürger's "Des Pfarrers Tochter von Taubenhain," the lover in his "Der wohlgesinnte Liebhaber," the girls in

Jakobi's two poems "Emma" and "Clärchen," Angelika and Clärchen in Klinger's "Faust," the infanticide in Maler Müller's "Das Nusskernen," the brown maiden in his poem by that name, the murderess in A. G. Meissner's poems "Lied einer Gefallenen" and "Die Mörderin," Luise in Schiller's "Die Kindesmörderin," Gretchen in Goethe's "Faust" and scores of others are forsaken girls, who are compelled to bear the burdens of an unmarried mother. Most of them, overwhelmed with shame and anxiety, kill the child of him who has abandoned them to their fate.

Very often the seducer had made promises to the girl to marry her or to care for her. In the civil courts, if an unmarried mother wanted to bring a successful suit against the illegitimate father of her child, she was compelled to produce a written contract of marriage signed by her former lover.[22] Bürger's poem "Der Ritter und sein Liebchen" contains the story of a deserted girl, who had been promised marriage. When the lover is about to leave her she naïvely says,

> Komm fein bald wieder heim in's Land,
> Dass uns umschling ein schönres Band,
> Als Band von Gold und Seide,
> Ein Band aus Lust und Freude,
> Gewirkt von Priesterhand!—

But the seducer frankly tells her that he no longer has any intention of marrying her. When he rides away, the girl realizes that she has been betrayed. The poem concludes

> Traut, Mädchen, leichten Rittern nicht!
> Manch Ritter ist ein Bösewicht,
> Sie löffeln wohl und wandern
> Von Einer zu der Andern,
> Und freien Keine nicht.

Rosette in "Des Pfarrers Tochter von Taubenhain," has also been promised marriage. In Schubart's poem "Hannchen an Wilhelm" the girl accuses Wilhelm thus:

[22] See Barkhausen in *Deutsches Museum*, 1776², p. 686. Hess' "Freymüthige Gedanken," p. 61f.

> Denk, wie du mir mit hohem Schwur
> Die Ehe hast versprochen,
> Ach, armer Wilhelm, denke nur,
> Gott lässt ja keinen falschen Schwur
> Auf Erden ungerochen.

But Lenz in particular employs this motif. We find it in his "Zerbin," where Hohendorf cannot propose to Miss Freundlach because a written promise of marriage is held by an imperial notary public in favor of an unmarried mother who was just then rearing one of his illegitimate children. Zerbin too promises to marry Marie after his father dies but his failure even to provide for her prompts her to get rid of the fruit of their forbidden love as soon as it comes to the world. Marie too in "Die Soldaten" has a promise of marriage which her father threatens to send to the parents of the seducer, Desportes, after he has deserted her.

Often the seducer resorted to perjury. Guntel in Maler Müller's "Das Nusskernen" laughs at Fröhlich's vows: "That may be for today, but what of tomorrow? April weather, men's vows. Today and tomorrow are two different days." A girl in Thümmel's "Reise in die mittäglichen Provinzen Frankreichs" speaks of men as "Wortbrüchiges Geschlecht." The motif of perjury reaches its climax in Sprickmann's "Ida," A. G. Meissner's two poems "Lied einer Gefallenen" and "Die Mörderin," Gemmingen's drama and Schiller's "Die Kindesmörderin." In the first of Meissner's poems the girl warns the unborn child not to inherit the characteristics of the father and then proceeds to tell what awaits it if it should be a girl.

> Dir wird ein Jüngling schmeicheln,
> mit süsser Lockung viel;
> wird schwören falsche Schwüre,
> denn Schwur ist Männerspiel.

In the second poem she returns to this theme

> Sie schmeckten so süsse
> die buhlenden Küsse!
> Sie waren des Meineids so voll!

In Gemmingen's drama the motif is again taken up. Lottchen goes to Amalia, the rich widow, selected for Karl's wife, to appeal to her sympathy. When she fails to get it, Lotte exclaims: "Let us see what right you have to Karl, if you are able to do anything against the vows which heaven has recorded against the wailings of a forsaken girl, against the whimpering of the creature which I am carrying under my heart." And the infanticide in Schiller's poem exclaims

> Seine Eide donnern aus dem Grabe wieder,
> Ewig, ewig würgt sein Meineid fort,

when she thinks of the time when Joseph promised to care for her. In a later stanza she recalls burning his letters and her happiness when they actually took fire:

> Glücklich! Glücklich! Seine Briefe lodern,
> Seine Eide frisst ein siegend Feu'r,
> Seine Küsse! wie sie hochauflodern!—
> Was auf Erden war mir einst so teu'r?

On Joseph's vows she had staked her whole future happiness and she had lost.

Lessing who was a prophet in so many ways to the writers of the Storm and Stress reveals his sympathy with the forsaken girl in "Emilia Galotti," where he lets Orsina say to Odoardo: "I am a woman, yet I came hither resolute. We, old man, can trust each other, for we are both injured, and by the same seducer. Oh, if you knew how preposterously, how inexpressibly, how incomprehensibly, I have been injured by him, you would almost forget his conduct towards yourself. Do you know me? I am Orsina, the deluded, forsaken Orsina—perhaps forsaken only for your daughter. But how is she to blame? Soon she also will be forsaken, then another, another and another. Ha! (as if in rapture) what a celestial thought! when all who have been victims of his arts shall form a band, and we shall be converted into Maenads, into furies; what transport will it be to tear him piecemeal, limb by limb, to wallow through his entrails, and wrench from its seat the traitor's heart—that heart which he promised to bestow on each, and gave to none. Ha! that indeed will be glorious revelry!"

Desertion naturally leads to hatred. Since the typical unmarried mother was a deserted girl it is not surprising to find many literary productions portraying the hatred of the girl for her seducer. Writers felt that this hatred was one of the motives which prompted the unmarried mother to become a murderess. And in order to justify this hatred and to show the intensity of it, writers contrasted the happy days of love-making with the later pitiful condition of the girl. Thümmel tells of a girl who had gone insane with despair after her lover deserted her. She recalls the happy days of yore:

> Als er sich mir, von allen
> Ihn Wünschenden, ergab,
> Mit welchem Wohlgefallen
> Sah Gott auf uns herab!
>
> Mein Auge nun von süssen
> Gefühlen überging,
> Und ich mit Erstlingsküssen
> An seinen Wangen hing.
>
> Und ich in seinen Blicken
> Mein Bild gezeichnet fand—

Suddenly she thinks of her present condition:

> Natur! war diess Entzücken
> Nur Blendwerk deiner Hand?
> *   *   *   *   *   *
> Kannst du auch Rache segnen?
> So nimm, Gott, meinen Schmerz
> Und grab ihn dem verwegnen
> Mordschuldigen ins Herz.

And then she goes into hysterics. Thümmel gives vent to his emotions in these words: "Every pulsation set her cheeks aglow with an increased redness, her bosom throbbed as if to burst, her long blond hair escaped its bonds, and fluttered gleaming like a comet through the night of her prison. . . .

She beat the air with her hands, with her bared arms, strength-
ened with rage, . . . I saw in her place an avenging angel,
who hovers over a potter's field and seeks out the bloody
traces of outraged innocence and virtue. Threats of eternity
flashed from her eyes, and flowed from her foaming lips."
The poet says he had no eyes, no more pity for the other
unfortunate inmates, his heart was so full of the soul-suffering
of this glorious woman, and he realized more than ever the
truth of her assertion:

> Um mich Zerknirschte sammeln
> Sich viel Bedrängte her
> Doch Aller Zungen stammeln:
> "Ach, diese leidet mehr!"

The hatred of the seducer is frequently brought about by
jealousy of another girl. Bürger's Rosette is told by the
Junker that he cannot marry her because of the difference of
rank. The girl replies

> Dass Gott dich,—du schändlicher, bübischer Mann!
> Dass Gott dich zur Hölle verdamme!—

A fisherman in Miller's "Siegwart" pulls the corpse of a
beautiful girl out of the Danube, while Kronhelm and Siegwart stand by. On her body they find a letter addressed to
Joseph: "You have made a nice mess of it, Joseph. You
promised to marry me, even swearing in the name of the Holy
Virgin that you would, and now you have taken another girl.
But I know what I shall do. . . . In the Danube many have
found their grave, I shall find mine there too." Hannchen
in Schubart's poem "Hannchen an Wilhelm" says:

> Ha, falscher Wilhelm! spottest mein,
> In deines Liebchens Armen,

and the pregnant girl in his "Das schwangere Mädchen"
likewise complains:

> Und nun eilt mit frecher Stirne
> In die Arme einer Dirne
> Der Verruchte, spottet, lacht,
> Dass er mich zu Fall gebracht.

Maler Müller's idyl "Das Nusskernen" tells of a girl who
kills her child from jealousy of another girl, who has supplanted
her. When she is in court, however, she refuses to divulge the
name of him who has brought her into trouble. Her refusal
later drives the seducer to confession. Marie in Lenz's
"Zerbin" likewise shields her seducer and dies without telling
his name. Zerbin is amazed at her nobility of soul and later
commits suicide. Luise in Schiller's poem reveals what she
thought when she killed her child:

> Ach vielleicht umflattert eine andre,
> Mein vergessen, dieses Schlangenherz,
> Überfliesst, wenn ich zum Grabe wandre,
> An dem Putztisch in verliebten Scherz!

A much more important motive which prompted the unmarried mother to become an infanticide was the fear of
shame. Justus Möser in looking over the 785 cases of illegitimacy referred to above, suggested that the fear of shame
was the first thing which came to the mind of a girl when she
discovered that she was about to become a mother. The
formula for the girls of the peasant class, so Möser asserted,
was: "O Jesus! Johann, wenn dar man niks van upsteit!"
and for those of the upper classes: "O Herr Gott! Wenn
etwas davon käme! Was wäre ich ein unglückliches Kind!
Was wollten Papa und Mama sagen!"

The ridicule of parents, especially that of the father, was
especially to be dreaded. Erich Schmidt in his excellent
characterization of the cruel father in Wagner's "Kindermörderinn" pointed out recurrences and imitations of this character in such a large number of productions of this and succeeding periods, that critical discussion recognizes "der pol-
ternde Vater" as a typical figure.

First of all there is the unrelenting father, who drives his
unfortunate daughter from home and maintains his cruel
attitude to the bitter end. Such a parent is the father of
Rosette in Bürger's "Des Pfarrers Tochter von Taubenhain."

> Der Vater, ein harter und zorniger Mann,
> Schalt laut die arme Rosette;

"Hast du dir erbuhlt für die Wiege das Kind,
So hebe dich mir aus den Augen geschwind,
Und schaff' auch den Mann dir in's Bette!"

Er schlang ihr fliegendes Haar um die Faust;
Er hieb sie mit knotigen Riemen.
*   *   *   *   *   *   *   *
Er stiess sie hinaus in der finstersten Nacht
Bei eisigem Regen und Winden.

Rosette never returns.

Humbrecht, in Wagner's "Die Kindermörderinn," is equally blustering but relents in the end. When he discovers that the "beautiful maid in the rear of the house" is a prospective unmarried mother, he shouts: "Das Lumpenzeug! der verdammte Nickel! Den Augenblick soll sie mir aus dem Haus. . . . Wirsts ihr bald ankündigen oder nicht? wenn ichs ihr selbst sagen muss, so steh ich nicht dafür, dass ich sie nicht mit dem Kopf zuerst die Treppen hinunterschmeiss." When he finds out that Evchen and her mother have been at the ball during his absence he blusters, then calms down and warns: "Diesmal sollst noch so durchschlupfen; Wenns aber noch einmal geschieht, Blitz und Donner! nur noch einmal, so tret ich dir alle Ribben im Leib entzwey." It is no wonder that such blustering drives Evchen from home when she discovers that she too is a prospective unmarried mother. The humanity of the father is revealed, however, in his persistent effort to locate his daughter after she has run away from home. After Evchen has killed her child in the last act of the drama the father suddenly appears on the scene. For a moment he is stunned by what he beholds, he veritably barks at the messengers of the court but at his departure he assures Evchen: "Adieu! Am armen Sünderhäussel seh ich dich wieder, Eve! Sag dir das letztemal Adieu!" In spite of all his severity, he is willing to perform his duty as father, by his presence to console her in the most excruciating ordeal of her life.

To this type also belong the fathers depicted in Lenz's dramas, and in his "Zerbin." The severity of the Major in

"Der Hofmeister" drives his daughter Gustchen from home, after she has been betrayed by Läuffer. After a prolonged search he finds her and weeps like a child because he is so happy to have her again. The two emotions which are most prominent are his natural tendency to severity on the one hand and his natural love for his child on the other. This contrast is best brought out in the last act. After the Major has rescued Gustchen from drowning, he says: "There! put her down, (he and the privy councillor try to encourage her) accursed child! did I have to educate you to this end! (kneels down beside her) Gustel! what is the matter? Have you swallowed some water? You are my Gustel anyhow, are you not? . . . Wicked good-for-nothing! If you had only said one word about it before; I would have bought a title of nobility for the rascal and you could have been married." Then she asks his pardon. He answers: "Yes, may the devil pardon you, degenerate child. No, (kneels down at her side) do not fall down my Gustel—my Gustel! I shall pardon you, everything is forgiven and forgotten. . . . O, you my only dearest treasure! I am so glad that I can carry you on my arms again, you wicked good-for-nothing!"

Another type of blustering father is the father who foresees the tragic possibilities of the girl's condition and does everything in his power to prevent them. Such a father is Walter in Maler Müller's idyls. Veitel, Lotte's sweetheart, is about to leave for an extended journey. The latter, expecting to be a mother soon, fears that something may happen in his absence which may make it impossible for them to be married; that he may never return or another girl may alienate his affections. The father of Lotte notices that she is very sad and rebukes her, whereupon the "Schulmeister" warns him to be careful lest he bring some misfortune to pass. He suddenly realizes the situation and immediately accedes to the desire of Veitel and Lotte to marry.

More than the ridicule of parents, unmarried mothers feared the ridicule of the world. Rosette in Bürger's "Des Pfarrers Tochter von Taubenhain" pleads with the Junker

> O mach' es nun gut, was du übel gemacht!
> Bist du es, der mich in Schande gebracht,
> So bring' auch mich wieder zu Ehren!—

When he refuses she curses him with the wish

> Dann fühle, Verräther, dann fühle, wie's thut,
> An Ehr' und an Glück zu verzweifeln!

The infanticide of whom Sturz tells in his essay "Ueber Linguets Vertheidigung der Todesstrafen" admits to the judges that she had a terrific struggle before she decided to kill her own child. "I lost my virtue," she relates, "and now my peace of life was gone. How they will look down upon me, ridicule my pride and my disgrace! How I shall be compelled to atone for this false step of a single minute all my long miserable life! Now I am no longer worthy of a girl friend, or of a husband, of the respect of my playmates, or even of a single pleasure. The honorable name of mother is an eternal title of disgrace for me. Oh my judges, such thoughts raged in my bosom in the hour of child-birth!"

No poet so strongly portrayed the unmarried mother's fear of the world's ridicule as did Goethe. We get an idea of the power of this ridicule in the scene "Am Brunnen," where Gretchen learns of the fall of Bärbelchen. Lieschen says of the latter:

> So ist's ihr endlich recht ergangen.
> * * * * * * *
> Da mag sie denn sich ducken nun,
> Im Sünderhemdchen Kirchbuss' tun!

Gretchen recalls how she formerly joined her playmates in heaping disgrace on a poor girl who had made a mistake, and then she sees the consequences of her own condition when she confesses

> Und bin nun selbst der Sünde bloss!

A little later she cries to the *mater dolorosa:*

> Hilf! rette mich von Schmach und Tod!

Not until Valentin as the representative of a cruel society pours out his venom against his sister, however, does this fear of the ridicule of the world come to full expression. Valentin says:

> Ich sag' dir's im Vertrauen nur:
> Du bist doch nun einmal eine Hur';
> So sei's auch eben recht.
> * * * * * * *
> Ich seh' wahrhaftig schon die Zeit,
> Dass alle brave Bürgersleut;
> Wie von einer angesteckten Leichen,
> Von dir, du Metze! seitab weichen.
> Dir soll das Herz im Leib verzagen,
> Wenn sie dir in die Augen sehn!
> * * * * * * *
> In eine finstre Jammerecken
> Unter Bettler und Krüppel dich verstecken,
> Und wenn dir dann auch Gott verzeiht,
> Auf Erden sei vermaledeit!

Not a word of pity, not one of forgiveness.

Then there was the fear of shame for the innocent child and the voluntary surrender of the girl to the law in order to expiate her deed. In Sturz's essay referred to above, the infanticide prays: "O Creator, take it, this innocent child, it will escape all the cares of a miserable life." Ida in Sprickmann's poem by the same name fears for the future of the child also.

> O Humfried! deiner Liebe Kind—
> Was soll, was soll ihm werden?
> Soll's, überall wo Menschen sind,
> Soll's auf dem weiten Rund der Erden,
> Mit der Mutter in Schande
> Verfluchen dich!
> Verfluchen mich!
> Verfluchen unsrer Liebe Bande?

In his "Mariens Reden bei ihrer Trauung" Sprickmann depicts the extremes to which a mother will go to give her child a chance in life. Marie, instead of killing her illegitimate child, summons Karl, the unmarried father, and insists that he fulfill his promise of marriage. After she has pleaded with him a long time without success, she takes poison to convince him of the seriousness of her demand. When he sees this he yields, the preacher and the witnesses who have been waiting in the adjoining room are called in, the ceremony is performed, but Marie before taking final leave of her now legal husband, says: "Karl, forgive me, it was only for the sake of the child!"

Lotte in Gemmingen's drama asks Karl in the letter she writes to him: "What shall a parentless child, a disgraced girl do in this world? If you forsake me I shall kill the child with my own hands and then let them execute me publicly." Schiller too felt the power of this motif. In "Die Kindes-mörderin" Luise thinks of the future when the child will ask

> Weib, wo ist mein Vater? lallte
> Seiner Unschuld stumme Donnersprach',

and the mother will answer,

> Weh, umsonst wirst, Waise, du ihn suchen,
> Der vielleicht schon andre Kinder herzt,
> Wirst der Stunde unsres Glückes fluchen,
> Wenn dich einst der Name Bastard schwärzt.[23]

The origin of the motive of fear of shame is to be found in the emphasis placed by the church on virginity at marriage. This emphasis is reflected in certain customs which obtained far and wide in Europe in the last half of the eighteenth century. There was the permission given to the chaste bride to wear a laurel wreath on her wedding-day, the celebration of the rose festival, in which only chaste maidens could take

---

[23] The motif is used by a number of authors before Schiller and is so similar in wording that one suspects borrowing. For instance the mother in Maler Müller's "Das braune Fräulein" says:

> Einst kämst du erwachsen:
> Wo, Mutter, ist der Mann,
> Den ich soll Vater nennen?
> Hab' ich kein Vater dann?

Cf. also A. G. Meissner's "Die Mörderin."

part, the crowning with a laurel wreath of young men and women, who had died chaste, or the placing of a wreath on their bier for the same reason, and the hanging of a straw wreath on the door of the home of a fallen girl. The prevalence of these customs is reflected in Goethe's "Faust," where Lieschen tells Gretchen of the fall of Bärbelchen:

> Das Kränzel reissen die Buben ihr,
> Und Häckerling streuen wir vor die Tür!

Or we find it in Maler Müller's "Das braune Fräulein," in which he depicts a girl who has been deserted by her lover after he has dishonored her. She meets him one day by chance and throws herself on his mercy; he however informs her that he cannot marry her, he has already promised another. She breaks out in lamentation:

> O führ' vor allen Augen,
> Im Hochzeitkranz beblümt,
> Mich aus der Jungfraun Kammer
> Wie's, Liebster, sich geziemt.

Another victim of seduction bewails her condition thus:

> O dass mein Püppchen in der Welt,
> Doch schon—im Schoos der Amme wär!
> Und ich!—ich arme, todt! dahin!
> Denn ich heiss doch nie Jungfer mehr.[24]

The personification of chastity as a blooming wreath, and the loss of it as a wilting one, is very widely used in this literature. A writer in the *Deutsches Museum* in a poem "Die Mode" sarcastically addresses a young rake:

> Ob du junger Unschuld Kränze raubst,
> Dir Betrug und Ehebruch erlaubst,
> *   *   *   *   *   *   *   *
> Das entehrt dich Erstgebornen nicht.

Lisel in Meissner's "Lied von der schwarzen Lise aus Kastilien" is asked by her mother why she is pining her life away. She tells how a young man had betrayed her.

[24] See *Taschenbuch für Dichter und Dichterfreunde*, IX, 80.

> Ach! ein Jüngling hat geschworen;
> Und sein Schwur ist fort.
> Ach! ein Jüngling hat geschworen;
> Und mein Kränzchen dorrt—

Kindleben in his "Studenten-Lexikon" defines "Jungfer" thus: "This kind of creature is said to be very rare even in the best circles. One therefore calls a girl after she is sixteen, in order not to offend the truth, "Jungfrau" or "junge Frau" or "Mamsell," as they call a "Junker" "junger Herr." Girls who were not married but had lost their virtue or even had a living witness of their forbidden love still insisted on being called "Jungfer." Thus Frau Marthan addresses Evchen, the unmarried mother in Wagner's "Die Kindermörderinn," by the term "Jungfer," to which the latter replies: "Are you addressing me, Frau Marthan?" Frau Marthan: "Whom else? Shall I not call you that? Curious! —there are so many of high and low degree about the city, who already support three and four such dolls as yours, and they would scratch your eyes out or bring suit against you in the courts, if you did not call them "Jungfer," after as well as before."

Pestalozzi revolted against all these customs which only intensified the girl's fear of disgrace. He suggested that they be abolished. Hippel and Möser, however, were heartily in favor of their retention. The former thought the wearing of the laurel wreath of great value in determining who was virtuous.[25]

Another motif of infanticide utilized by poets was despair. Bürger's Rosette kills her child in a fit of despair.

> Erst, als sie vollendet die blutige That,
> Musst'! ach! ihr Wahnsinn sich enden.

The fallen girl in Meissner's "Das Lied einer Gefallenen" warns the unborn child,

> Nun bringe nicht die Züge
> des Vaters mit zur Welt!

[25] See Hippel, "Sämmtliche Werke," V, 223f.; Möser, "Patriotische Phantasien," 1842, V, 107f.

Weil mich sonst leicht Verzweiflung
allmächtig überfällt.

The old woman in Brentano's "Vom braven Kasperl und dem schönen Annerl" says of Annerl's deed: "She did it in her confusion. . . . Then she despaired and did the evil thing."[26] Thümmel tells of another infanticide who murdered her child "out of despair."[27] The artist in Gemmingen's drama points out the intense despair in the facial expression of the unfortunate girl on the first sketch he shows Karl, and later he says he would dislike much to be the prince who, on arriving in the other world, should be compelled to meet all the known and unknown murderesses who would come to meet him "despairingly." Luise in Schiller's poem is ruled by two powers: love and the madness of despair. And Faust reproaches Mephistopheles in Goethe's drama: "In misery! Despairing! Wandering miserably on the earth a long time and now imprisoned!"

Writers of this period entirely left out of consideration the physical explanation for the forebodings and fear which pregnant women have. Such forebodings were still looked upon as signs of a guilty conscience. The fears of the unmarried mother were always explained that way. Until the middle of the eighteenth century unmarried motherhood was often brought into connection with witchcraft. During the prevalence of this temporary insanity, which swept the whole of Europe and even extended to our own land, many a girl was executed because it was thought she had had commerce with the devil. It is no wonder that when such ideas were current the unmarried mother was thought to have such forebodings as a punishment for her sins.

The utilization of superstition is usually centered about execution and death, as well as the reward after death. Bürger was particularly clever in the use of superstition in his ballads. In "Des Pfarrers Tochter von Taubenhain" he makes good use of this motif. In the very first stanza an uncanny feeling comes over the reader.

[26] "Gesammelte Schriften," VI, 102.
[27] "Sämmtliche Werke," VI, 102.

Im Garten des Pfarrers von Taubenhain
Geht's irre bei Nacht in der Laube.
Da flistert und stöhnt's so ängstiglich;
Da rasselt, da flattert und sträubet es sich,
Wie gegen den Falken die Taube.

After he has told the process of the tragedy, he returns to the fated arbor. Rosette has just killed her child. She digs a grave for it with her own hands and bids farewell to it with the fateful words: Mich hacken die Raben vom Rade! Then we are to imagine that the execution of Rosette has taken place.

Das ist das Flämmchen am Unkenteich;
Das flimmert und flammert so traurig,
Das ist das Plätzchen, da wächst kein Gras;
Das wird vom Thau und vom Regen nicht nass;
Da wehen die Lüftchen so schaurig!

Allnächtlich herunter vom Rabenstein,
Allnächtlich herunter vom Rade,
Huscht bleich und wolkigt ein Schattengesicht,
Will löschen das Flämmchen, und kann es doch nicht,
Und wimmert am Unkengestade.

It was just this element of superstitition which made the poem popular. Heinrich Pröhle tells of a place in Pansfelde, the early home of Bürger, where an infanticide was supposed to have spent many hours on her hands and knees in supplication to God that her sins might be forgiven. It was not far from a parsonage where just such superstitious sounds and signs as Bürger recorded in his poem could be heard and seen. One sees how the poem affected the minds of the people. The transformation of the poem into a folk-song as it is reproduced in "Des Knaben Wunderhorn" is further evidence to the same end.

Often the superstitious element comes in the form of some foreboding, or dream. Thus Bürger's "Des armen Suschen's Traum" pictures a deserted girl, similar in some respects to "Lenore." Suschen tells of a dream,

Ich träumte, wie um Mitternacht
Mein Falscher mir erschien.
*   *   *   *   *   *   *

Er zog den Treuring von der Hand
Und ach! zerbrach ihn mir.
Ein wasserhelles Perlenband
Warf er mir hin dafür.

Then in a later stanza she tells us

Erfüllt ist längst das Nachtgesicht,
Ach! längst erfüllt genau.
*   *   *   *   *   *   *

Nun brich, o Herz, der Ring ist hin!
Die Perlen sind geweint!
Statt Myrt' erwuchs dir Rosmarin!
Der Traum hat Tod gemeint.

Jung-Stilling in "Heinrich Stillings Jugend und Jünglings-jahre" tells of a melancholic girl who had a very peculiar foreboding of her future lot. The girl had a dream in which she went out on a meadow. Here she was suddenly approached by a young man, who accosted her and then was changed into a ghost. The ghost directed that she should look in a certain direction, where she beheld a poor unmarried mother, clad in rags from head to foot, with a small child on her arm, which looked very miserable. Then the ghost said: "See! this is already the third illegitimate child, that you shall have." The girl fainted away and when she awoke she lay in her bed bathed in cold perspiration. In the next paragraph the author reports that the sad life of the girl proved that the dream came true. A year after she had dreamed she committed her first folly, which was only the first step to her fall. She was later compelled to stand in stocks before the public and be ridiculed as an arch-harlot. The relating of the incident ends in a polemic against laws which forced the unmarried mother to become an outcast of society.

Writers cleverly utilized the remorse of the unfaithful lover after the girl's death. They interpret the pangs of his conscience as the torment which the girl inflicts after she has departed this life. In her utter helplessness the girl finds comfort in her belief that there will be a day of reckoning, and that she will have an opportunity to pursue her unfaithful sweetheart as a spirit. Thus the girl who commits suicide in Miller's "Siegwart" warns Joseph: "Be careful! I invite you to come to the valley of Josaphat on the first day of the new year." Hannchen in Schubart's poem "Hannchen an Wilhelm" threatens,

> Doch wisse nur, Gott wird sich mein
> Am jüngsten Tag erbarmen.
> *   *   *   *   *   *   *
> Ach Wilhelm, Wilhelm, denke dran!
> Mein Geist wird dir erscheinen.

The lover in Maler Müller's "Das braune Fräulein," after wandering over the earth in an attempt to find peace, exclaims:

> Ja süsses, sanftes Mädchen
> Aus Treue starbst du, ach!
> Muss grausam dir nun folgen,
> Dein Geist, er winket nach!

Hölty in "Adelstan und Röschen" depicts the appearance of the spirit of the dead girl to her unfaithful lover:

> Sie zeigte, wann es zwölfe schlug,
> Jetzt alle Nächte sich,
> Verhüllet in ein Todtentuch,
> Und wimmert' und entwich.

The appearance of three spirits to Horry in Sprickmann's dramatic sketch by the same name, has already been alluded to. Schiller's Luise warns her seducer

> Joseph! Joseph! Auf entfernte Meilen
> Folge dir Luisens Totenchor,
> Und des Glockenturmes dumpfes Heulen
> Schlage schrecklich mahnend an dein Ohr—
> *   *   *   *   *   *   *   *   *
> Joseph! Joseph! Auf entfernte Meilen

> Jage dir der grimme Schatten nach,
> Mög' mit kalten Armen dich ereilen,
> Donnre dich aus Wonneträumen wach,
> Im Geflimmer sanfter Sterne zucke
> Dir des Kindes grasser Sterbeblick,
> Es begegne dir im blut'gen Schmucke,
> Geissle dich vom Paradies zurück!

There are two other motifs which are so typical in this literature as to merit attention. The first is the hell-motif. Hölty in "Adelstan und Röschen" lets the spirit of the girl pursue the unhappy Adelstan until he totters out to the cemetery and stabs himself.

> Folg'! ruft ein Teufel, folg'!
> Und seine Seel' entfährt.

Thümmel in telling of the insane unmarried mother lets her curse her lover,

> Durch Blutgefilde treibe
> Hinüber ihn mein Fluch,
> Und Satans Finger schreibe
> Ihn in sein Höllenbuch!

Ida in Sprickmann's poem feels the pangs of hell, when she addresses her child in the words

> Ha! Kaum noch da, und donnert nicht schon
> Des ersten Winselns Jammerton
> Der sterbenden Mutter den Höllenlohn?

and when she discovers the similarity of features of her child and of Humfried, she shrieks in rage

> Hölle!—Humfried's du!
> Und habe dich im Schoos?—Zum Teufel!—Hu!—Hu!—

In his dramatic sketch the third spirit says to Horry: "Teufel! Du hast Fülle in deinen Lenden; weiche Rosenbette hat die Hölle. Denk an Johannisnacht, und komm nach, mein Trauter! Wir wollen uns in den Flammen umarmen." And the murderess in Meissner's "Die Mörderin" exclaims

101

Welch schallender Jubel ertönt
Vom Höllenschlund empor?
Erschein, erschein, verfluchtes Chor!
Hol im Triumfe
zum höllischen Sumpfe
Die Mörderin, die deine Qualen höhnt!

Later she directs herself to her unfaithful lover:

Ha! zage, Verruchter!
Verzeiht Er nicht mir;
Dann bin ich, Verfluchter,
bald flammend bei dir.
Und schlepp dich zur Hölle
mit glühender Faust,
wo ewig dein Jammer
wie Wintersturm braust.

At bottom this motif is the girl's fear of damnation in hell.
Gretchen attempts to put aside her forebodings of this damnation, which the choir, in the scene "Dom" in "Faust,"
as the representative of the sanctimonious church heralds
forth. The evil spirit, a composite of the popular interpre-
tation of church decrees and of Gretchen's conscience, a spirit
which had prompted many another girl in Gretchen's pathetic
condition to try to conform to the demand of church and state,
namely to remain chaste in their sight, now dictates to her:

Verbirg dich! Sünd' und Schande
Bleibt nicht verborgen.

but warns at the same time

Und dein Herz
Aus Aschenruh
Zu Flammenqualen
Wieder aufgeschaffen,
Bebt auf!

Her only hope was in concealment of her condition and in the
clandestine destruction of her child. In the prison scene we

discover that she has failed in her attempt. When **Faust** comes to rescue her, her fear of damnation in hell is clearly brought to view by her words:

> O lass uns knien, die Heil'gen anzurufen!
> Sieh! unter diesen Stufen,
> Unter der Schwelle
> Siedet die Hölle!
> Der Böse,
> Mit furchtbarem Grimme,
> Macht ein Getöse!

and a little later she adds

> Mitten durchs Heulen und Klappen der Hölle,
> Durch den grimmigen, teuflischen Hohn
> Erkannt ich den süssen, den liebenden Ton!

It is no wonder that Goethe later said of "Faust": "Ja, es ist etwas von der Hölle darin."

It must not be supposed, however, that the extensive use of the hell-motif indicates that all the writers still agreed with public opinion that every unmarried mother was damned. Lenz, for instance, lets Zerbin brood for days over the heroism of Marie during her trial and execution for clandestine childbirth. Finally Zerbin decides to put an end to his life, but before doing so he addresses a long prayer to the departed Marie in which he calls her a saint. In the concluding remarks of the novelette the author makes it clear that both the supposed infanticide and the suicide were saved. While the "Urfaust" of Goethe does not contain the words: "Sie ist gerettet!" a careful reading of the fragment can lead to no other conclusion than that Goethe intended that Gretchen should be saved.

The other motif is the eternal feminine. In order to make her tragedy more effective and to prove her innocence, Goethe portrays Gretchen as a typical representative of her sex. Her naïveté, her simplicity, her sincerity and her naturally willing surrender to the man ruled solely by passion, win the favor of the reader from the outset. The happy days of love-making form one of the most typical of human experiences. Even after her fall, Gretchen can never forget those happy days so full of bliss. In the prison scene she hears the voice of Faust and she happily exclaims:

> Er ist's! Er ist's! Wohin ist alle Qual?
> Wohin die Angst des Kerkers? der Ketten?
> Du bist's! Kommst mich zu retten!
> Ich bin gerettet!—
> Schon ist die Strasse wieder da,
> Auf der ich dich zum ersten Male sah.

Later she recalls those days again:

> Das war ein süsses, ein holdes Glück!

Another truly feminine and at the same time typically human trait is the willingness of the girl to sacrifice her life in expiation of her crime. Even Lenz and Wagner discovered the dramatic force of this trait. Evchen in "Die Kindermörderinn" insists that she must die, in fact she prefers to die. When the Magister pleads with her to marry Gröningseck, asserting that the latter has requested her to do so, she answers: "Me?—I swear he is no longer of any concern to me in this life. . . . And even if he wants to marry me ten times over, I would rather see the executioner." When Gröningseck proposes to go to Versailles to get a pardon she rebukes him: "Pardon for me? Gröningseck, what are you thinking of? —shall I die ten thousand deaths? I would rather die today than tomorrow." Marie in Lenz's "Zerbin" exclaims to her father: "I swear it, no human being dies more willingly than I do." Luise in Schiller's poem welcomes the messenger of the criminal court:

> Freudig eilt' ich, in dem kalten Tode
> Auszulöschen meinen Flammenschmerz.

When Faust comes to free Gretchen, she refuses to go with him because she wants to expiate her crime. When Faust pleads:

> Fühlst du, dass ich es bin, so komm!

She answers:

> Ist das Grab drauss!
> Lauert der Tod, so komm!
> Von hier ins ewige Ruhebett
> Und weiter keinen Schritt—
> *   *   *   *   *   *   *   *   *
> Ich darf nicht fort; für mich ist nichts zu hoffen.

And then there is the willingness to forgive. In spite of the hatred she has harbored in her soul against Joseph, Luise in Schiller's poem finally reveals her nobility of soul.

> Joseph!   Gott im Himmel kann verzeihen,
> Dir verzeiht die Sünderin.
> Meinen Groll will ich der Erde weihen.

Goethe goes even farther. He does not permit Gretchen to say one word of hatred against Faust. Faust remains her lover to the end. It is this unfathomable love which in the end saves him. Her "Heinrich! Heinrich!" at the end of Part I is not a reproach, but her last greeting of love, her invitation to save his soul as she has saved hers. This explains her joy at the end of Part II when Faust's soul is borne to heaven by the hands of angels.

> Neige. neige,
> Du Ohnegleiche,
> Du Strahlenreiche,
> Dein Antlitz gnädig meinem Glück!
> Der früh Geliebte,
> Nicht mehr Getrübte,
> Er kommt zurück.

CHAPTER IV

CONCLUDING OBSERVATIONS

Eduard Engel in his "Geschichte der deutschen Literatur" voices the opinion of a great many critics when he refers to Zimmermann's assertion that the writers of the Storm and Stress period were "'Kraftknaben,' who wanted to revolutionize the whole of Germany and were not able to drive out a single fly."[1] This attitude toward the results of the revolt against conditions which increased unmarried motherhood and consequent infanticide is based on a wrong supposition, namely, that the revolt was carried on by a few 'stormy' youths, the 'original geniuses.' It was not that the 'original geniuses' carried on a revolt but that the extensive revolt found one of its forms of expression in the productions of the 'original geniuses.' Quite naturally the results of the agitation have not been sought heretofore in law-books and other non-esthetic literature.

What were some of these results? Capital punishment of infanticides had been abolished in Russia before 1770. In 1775 it was also abolished in parts of Austria Hungary. It was not until Pestalozzi became known to the rulers of Austria that reform legislation was pushed to its conclusion. De Guimps, an American critic of the great educator, writes: "As early as the second number of the *Schweizer-Blatt*, 1782, there is a fragment of an essay on infanticide, which, together with his other writings, attracted the attention of the most distinguished princes of the time. The Emperor Joseph II, for instance, and the Grand Duke of Tuscany, both endeavored to apply Pestalozzi's views to the improvement of the condition of their subjects, and particularly to the reform of penal legislation and of prison discipline, and with this object instructed their ministers to communicate with the author of "Leonard and Gertrude."[2]

[1] Leipzig, 1907, II, 567. Cf. also 569.
[2] Roger de Guimps, "Pestalozzi." New York, 1890, p. 90.

In Schlözer's *Stats-Anzeigen* we read that in Austria, after January 13, 1787, capital punishment was only imposed on the ringleaders of public mobs. In all other cases it was abolished.[3] In Bavaria this punishment for infanticide was not entirely abolished until 1813, but in looking over the records of the criminal courts one rarely finds an instance of capital punishment after 1790. Generally infanticides were sentenced to imprisonment. The same may be said of the other provinces of Germany. While capital punishment was not officially abolished until later, it was seldom decreed in practice after 1790. In Sweden the king admitted that capital punishment did not prevent the commission of infanticide and therefore decreed that after April 12, 1779, infanticides should no longer be executed but be imprisoned instead.[4] His other decrees in regard to the care of the unmarried mother and her child are equally interesting and show the influence of the agitation. In England the conditions under which capital punishment was to be decreed were greatly modified in 1775.[5]

Torture had been abolished in Prussia in 1740. In Austria it was abolished in 1776. Its abolition was attributed to the untiring efforts of a man of merit and talent, a professor of political economy in the University of Vienna. He in turn was influenced by Beccaria.[6] In Sweden torture was abolished in 1772 and in the Palatinate of Bavaria in 1779.[7]

Church penance for infanticides was abolished in Prussia in 1746, in Russia in 1766, in Austria soon thereafter by Maria Theresa. In Sweden it was abolished in 1779. Duke Karl August abolished it in the duchies of Weimar and Eisenach in 1786. Kindleben in his "Studenten-Lexikon" speaks of public church penance for infanticides as having received or as receiving the *consilium abeundi* in all the provinces of Germany.

The old law which required every unmarried mother to produce a written contract signed by the seducer, generally

[3] XII, 30.
[4] See Schlözer's *Briefwechsel*, V, 41ff.
[5] See Hess, "Freymüthige Gedanken," p. 237.
[6] Schlözer's *Briefwechsel*, I, 23f.
[7] *Idem*, IV, 233 and VI, 214.

called the *promesse de marriage*, was abolished in Prussia, and a new law was substituted in 1794. This new law gave unmarried mothers the rights of a legal mother and forced the seducer to marry her, if it was possible.[8] The numerous drafts of new codes of laws which were made in the 80's and 90's of the eighteenth century are, however, the most important evidence that the revolt had direct results.

These are all very definite visible results which can be found in the legal and social codes of that time. A further idea of the far-reaching effect of the revolt can be had from a reading of the literature of the period. It is evident that the attitude toward the fallen girl was changing from one of utter abhorrence to one of pity, even if this pity did not always express itself in acts. Maternity houses and homes of refuge for the unmarried mother were established everywhere in Europe. The illegitimate child was accepted into the community of church and state, into trades and unions, after it had been barred from such privileges for centuries. The interest in the illegitimate child is evidenced by the establishment of a large number of foundling-houses, and the efforts of some people, Pestalozzi for instance, to place the bastard child in private homes, where it would receive the same care as a legitimate child and thus be made a fit member of society. It is in the last half of the eighteenth century that we find the origin of our modern interest in the problem of the unmarried mother and her illegitimate child.

It is certain that most of the writers of the period consciously wished by their writings to make a contribution to the revolt against conditions which facilitated unmarried motherhood and consequent infanticide. Thus Gemmingen in "Der deutsche Hausvater," after letting the artist ascribe the frequency of infanticide to antiquated laws and to the cruelty of princes, lets him say: "I should dislike very much to be in the place of the prince, who, when he arrives in the other world, will be greeted by all the known and the unknown murderesses."[9] Wagner in defending the crass realism in "Die

---

[8] *Allgemeines Landrecht für die preussischen Staaten*, Berlin, 1832, IV, 614. Cf. Wainlud, "Die Kindstötung," p. 25f.

[9] Cf. *supra*, p. 96.

Kindermörderinn" says that he did not write his drama for the stage but for thoughtful readers.

In some cases the results of the efforts of writers can be instanced. The case of Pestalozzi has already been alluded to. In writing his essay the educator hoped that he might be used by some ruler to the end of changing conditions which made unmarried motherhood possible. Goethe, so Suphan states, was busied from 1778 on with the abolition of public church penance of unmarried mothers in the duchies of Eisenach and Weimar, and its abolition by Duke Karl August a few years later must be attributed in large part to the poet's activities. And in "Dichtung und Wahrheit" Goethe tells us that he "had seen so many families who had either been ruined by bankruptcies, divorces, seduced daughters, murders, robberies, poisonings, or miserably were clinging to the edge of existence," and that he had, young as he was, "often offered assistance in such cases."[10] Lenz in writing his essay "Ueber die Soldatenehen" makes a direct appeal to the rulers of the time, and hopes to be appointed to eradicate some of the evils which increased illegitimacy. Although the essay was not published until recently, it reveals Lenz's state of mind. In comparing the decrees of the king of Sweden and Hess' "Freymüthige Gedanken" one cannot fail to detect the influence of the latter on the former. From Laukhard's "Der Wild und Rheingraf Carl Magnus" we infer that the abolition of public church penance in the Rhenish provinces was brought about largely through the influence of a writer at the court of the count.

Results due to direct personal efforts and to the effectiveness of non-esthetic literature are therefore attested. In considering the effect of the imaginative literature of the period we must keep in mind that it had a two-fold aim; first, it attempted to influence public opinion in favor of sympathy for the unmarried mother; second, it was to become a contribution to the esthetic literature of the country and the world. I believe that in the first aim the writers succeeded fairly well while in the second they failed. The best evidence we have

[10] Weimarer Ausgabe XXVII, 113.

for believing that the influence of this literature was great on public opinion is the popularity of a number of productions. Bürger's "Des Pfarrers Tochter von Taubenhain," for example, became so popular with the people of a part of Germany that it soon became a folk-song and was included as such in "Des Knaben Wunderhorn" under the title "Des Pfarrers Tochter von Taubenheim." Schiller's "Die Kindesmör-derin" had a similar fate, except that instead of one populari-zation Erk and Böhme's collection of folk-songs brings seven variations of the popular form of Schiller's rather long poem. What is more, these variations were sung over the length and breadth of Germany for more than two decades. And why did the Berlin police forbid the staging of Wagner's "Die Kinder-mörderinn"? Certainly it can not be attributed to the danger that the players would be compelled to play to an empty house. It cannot be proved that the grossness which is so evi-dent in these productions kept people from reading them or that they failed to influence public opinion.

When we come to consider these productions as esthetic literature quite a different story is to be told. Justus Möser in passing criticism on the essay of Frederick the Great, entitled "Essay on the German language and literature," said: "Even the Klingers, the Lenzes and the Wagners in some respects showed the strength of Hercules." The greatest of the conservative jurists of the last half of the eighteenth century hereby recognized the literary merit of those who helped to abolish the evils which drove unmarried mothers to infanticide. After a century and a half the most truly dra-matic treatment of the theme of unmarried motherhood termi-nating in infanticide, the Gretchen tragedy in Goethe's "Faust," still continues to appeal to readers the world over. In Germany today this literary production is second only to the Bible in popularity. And this poetic treatment was born out of the travail of the revolt. And there are—just as Möser asserted—scenes, stanzas or passages in the other productions of the period which could be read universally with keen literary pleasure. The portrayal of the emotions which drove un-married mothers to infanticide belongs to the most stupendous of literary undertakings. The fear of the ridicule of parents, of friends, of church and state, of damnation in hell, despair coupled with a state of mind which was filled with superstition, jealousy of another girl, the dark outlook for the future of the illegitimate child, the prospect of being the greatest outcast of society, where in all literature is material more truly dramatic than this? And such emotions were portrayed with considerable skill by the writers of the Storm and Stress and in this we find the only reason for believing that their writings exerted a beneficent influence.

But with the exception of Goethe's "Faust"—the work of an immortal artist, whose superior artistry may well be taken for granted—all the literature on the unmarried mother, which I reviewed in the preceding chapter, has been forgotten. It is used only as material for scholarly investigation. Cultured Germans do not now think of reading Schiller's "Die Kindesmörderin," or Bürger's "Des Pfarrers Tochter von Taubenhain" and much less Sprickmann's "Ida" for purely literary pleasure. Even in the days of the Storm and Stress sensible people, while realizing fully the seriousness of the fact of infanticide and the necessity of correcting the agencies which facilitated it, nevertheless revolted against the misuse of poetic license. Why else should Boie write to Lenz when the latter's "Die Soldaten" came out: "I—you will laugh at me— think that the colors are too glaring here and there." Or why did Schubart change the title of his poem "Das schwangere Mädchen" to "Minchen am Grabe ihrer Mutter," and in the revision leave out all the gross elements? Or why did Sprickmann throw overboard his plan of a drama in which the crying babe was to send home the terrified audience with its pitiful wailing and substitute a drama, "Der Schmuck," with its peaceable solution? Or why was it necessary at all for Wagner and Klinger to defend the use of so much grossness in their productions? There is reason to believe that even Schiller's "Die Kindesmörderin" was the product of mistaken ideas about tragic art. For in 1805, when the drawings by Schnorr were shown to him he said: "They all meet with my approval except that one of the infanticide, which I cannot approve because of the subject-matter." The drawing brought out clearly the youthful poet's mistake in placing too much emphasis on the horrifying elements in the execution motif.

Most of the writers of this period failed to realize that the disgusting and horrible, while they are to be found in real life, when emphasized can never be effective art. The province of art is to attract, to ennoble, to lift up, to emphasize the beautiful, not to repel, to drag down, to debase, to stress the horrible. Enduring art, it is true, always reveals the spirit of the age in which it was produced, but it is well to remember that the emphasis is placed on the spirit and not on the portrayal of the repellent and offensive details. Writers of the Storm and Stress mistook the province of art, they even failed to understand human nature which, when sublimity is sought, always rebels against the exposition of the gross and the horrible. With Goethe it was different. He was able so to portray the tragedy of Gretchen as to make it attractive to readers the world over, he enlisted the sympathy of men and inspired them with the noble purpose of lifting up hapless unmarried mothers by emphasizing the beauty and sanctity of motherhood, be it married or unmarried. He portrayed the emotions of an unmarried mother, he did not give a minute description of repulsive details. In short Goethe embodied in the Gretchen tragedy the sympathy of the eighteenth century for a creature who had been wronged for more than a thousand years. This in part at least explains why of all the many productions of the Storm and Stress his alone has survived and has become a contribution to world literature.

BIBLIOGRAPHY

The following bibliography includes the literature on unmarried motherhood, using the term literature in the broader sense, of the period 1770–1800, and the literature which was used to get the necessary background for an understanding of the history and development of the revolt. With a few exceptions only the literature which could be had in this country is listed, therefore no claim to completeness of the list of productions on unmarried motherhood during this period is made.

Abegg, "Beiträge zur Geschichte der Strafrechtspflege in Schlesien im 15. und 16. Jahrhundert." In *Zeitschrift für deutsches Recht*, Tübingen, XVIII, 423f.

"Ueber das Erforderniss der Lebensfähigkeit bei dem Thatbestande der Kindstötung mit Rücksicht auf die neueren Strafgesetzgebungen." In the same magazine, XIX.

Adelung, J. C., "Ueber den Deutschen Styl." Berlin, 1785, II, 149.

Alemannia, XVIII, 52, "Erinnerung an Jus Talionis. Motiv von der littauischen Kindermörderin." XXVII, 247–297, "Die Kindermorde zu Benzhausen und Waldkirch im Breisgau. Ein Gedicht aus dem Anfang des 16. Jahrhunderts."

Allgemeine Deutsche Bibliothek, Berlin und Stettin.

 72, 374: Aepli, "Mittel wider den Kindermord."

 48, 95: "Das beste ausführbare Mittel wider den Kindermord." Dresden, 1781.

 66, 89: *Die neue Gometz.* II, Part 3, Leipzig, 1785.

 63, 81: "Drei Preisschriften über die Frage: Welche sind die besten ausführbarsten Mittel, dem Kindermorde abzuhelfen, ohne die Unzucht zu begünstigen." Mannheim bey Schwan, 1784.

 54, 109: "Fragmente über die Frage: Welches sind

die besten ausführbaren Mittel, dem Kindermord Einhalt zu thun?" Frankfurt und Leipzig, 1782.

52, 478: "Freymüthige Gedanken über die Frage: Welches sind die besten ausführbaren Mittel dem Kindermord Einhalt zu thun? Göttingen, 1781.

58, 75: "Freymüthige Gedanken, Wünsche und Vorschläge eines vaterländischen Bürgers über den Kindermord, und die Mittel denselben zu verhindern, Teutschlands Söhnen und Töchtern gewidmet. Germanien, 1783.

48, 96: Von Hess, Ludwig, "Eine Antwort auf die Preisfrage: Welches sind die besten ausführbaren Mittel dem Kindermorde Einhalt zu thun?" Hamburg, 1780.

54, 175: Irwing, K. F., "Fragment der Naturmoral, oder Betrachtungen über die natürlichen Mittel der Glückseligkeit, bey Gelegenheit der Mannheimer Preisaufgabe über die Mittel, dem Kindermord Einhalt zu tun." Berlin, 1782.

61, 93: Kärner, "Bittschrift der unehelich erzeugten Bürger Teutschlands an die teutsche Landesherrn." 1783.

59, 395: List, G. D. K., "Ueber Hurerey und Kindermord." Mannheim, 1784.

52, 478: May, F., "Vorbeugungsmittel wider den Kindermord, für Seelsorger, Eltern, Polizeyverwalter, usw." Mannheim, 1781.

Anhang I to 37–52, 126: Müller, K., "Mittel wider den Kindermord. Eine Beantwortung der Mannheimer Preisaufgabe." Halle, 1781.

66, 380: "Nachtrag zu den Abhandlungen über die besten ausführbaren Mittel, dem Kindermord Einhalt zu thun." Tübingen, 1782.

54, 113: "Noch eine Meinung über die Frage: Welches sind die besten ausführbaren Mittel, dem Kindermord Einhalt zu thun." Tübingen, 1783.

52, 478: Patsch, "Beantwortung der Preisfrage: Welches sind die besten ausführbaren Mittel dem Kindermorde Einhalt zu thun ohne die Unzucht zu begünstigen?" 1781.

60, 109: Pestalozzi, J. H., "Ueber Gesetzgebung und Kindermord." Frankfurt und Leipzig, 1783.

88, 90: Pfeil, J. G. B., "Preisschrift von den besten und ausführbarsten Mitteln, dem Kindermord abzuhelfen, ohne die Unzucht zu begünstigen, mit Zusätzen und einem sechsfachen Anhang dahin einschlagender Materien." Leipzig, 1788.

85, 155f.: "Räsonnements, Paradoxen, Charaktere, Projecten und Vorreden ohne Buch." Berlin, 1786.

113, 55f.: Rathlef, E. L. M., "Vom Geiste der Criminalgesetze." Bremen, 1790.

67, 404: "Reflektionen über Schwängerung, Hurkinder und Ehelosigkeit des 18ten Jahrhunderts." 1785.

48, 98: Spörl, C. C., "Beantwortung der Mannheimischen Preisfrage: Welches sind die besten ausführbaren Mittel dem Kindermorde Einhalt zu thun?" Mühlhausen, 1781.

54, 112: Schlegel, G., "Mittel zur Verhütung des Kindermords, bey Gelegenheit der Mannheimischen Aufgabe und zur allgemeinen Beförderung der Tugend, mit andern die Sittlichkeit und Strafen betreffenden Betrachtungen aufgesezt." Dessau und Leipzig, 1783.

52, 150f.: Schwager, J. M., "Beyträge zur Bildung deutscher Bürger, in lehrreichen und unterhaltenden Aufsätzen." Leipzig, 1781.

62, 70: Von Soden, J. F., "Geist der teutschen Criminalgesetze." Dessau, 1783.

54, 92: "Ueber den Kindermord. Hingeworfene Gedanken eines Nichtfacultisten." Frankfurt am Mayn, 1782.

62, 304: "Ueber Empfindeley und Kraftgenies, Modevorurtheile und Schimpfreden, auch einige ernste Gegenstände." I, 3, Dessau und Leipzig, 1783.

72, 609: Veltusen, J. C., "Beyträge über Kindermord, usw." Wien, 1785.

54, 111: "Versuche über die Mittel wider den Kindermord. Auf Veranlassung der Mannheimer Preisfrage. Von einem Kriminalrichter." Berlin und Stralsund, 1782.

52, 478: "Versuch über die Beantwortung der Preisfrage: Welches sind etc." Nürnberg, 1781.

Cf. also Anhang to 37–52, 128.

47, 306: "Von den Mitteln dem Kindermord Einhalt zu thun."

47, 306: "Von den Strafen der Geschwächten." Published in *Schwäbisches Magazin von gelehrten Sachen*. 1780.

57, 102: "Von Strafen unehelicher Schwängerungen, usw." Erlangen, 1783.

79, 406: "Vom Kindermord und dessen Verhütung." Frankfurt und Leipzig, 1787.

57, 142: "Vorschläge einiger Mittel zur Verhütung des Kindermords, als Beantwortung der deshalb von einem Menschenfreunde vorgelegten Preisfrage." Leipzig, 1783.

66, 286: Discussion of an article on infanticide by Wekhrlin in *Der Chronolog*, XI and XII, 1781.

Allgemeine Literatur Zeitung, Jena, 1790. July 5, III, 41, "Kindermord nicht Kindermord." A review of an article in *Almanach für Aerzte und Nichtaerzte auf das Jahr 1790*.

Anonymous, "Aufgefangene Nonnenbriefe. Mit einem Anhange-Charlotte im Kerker, eine gefühlvolle Scene." 1779. Cf. *Allgemeine Deutsche Bibliothek*, 41, 459. I was unable to obtain this production.

Anzeiger für Kunde der deutschen Vorzeit, 1853, 95; 1854, 114; 1855, 176.

Archiv des Criminalrechts. Herausgegeben von E. F. Klein und G. A. Kleinschrod. Halle, 1798–1849. "Actenmässige Geschichte einiger Kindesmörderinnen" runs through a series of volumes. See especially I, II, III.

H. L. W. B., "Abgekürzte Reflexionen über den Nuzen oder Schaden der Todesstrafen." In *Deutsches Museum*, 1776[2], 947.

Barkhausen, Viktor, "Ueber Abschaffung der Todesstrafen." In *Deutsches Museum*, 1776[2], 667ff.

"Erläuterungen über die Todesstrafen." In *Deutsches Museum*, 1777[2], 336ff.

Beccaria, Cesare Bonesana Marchese di, "Dei delitti e delle pene." English translation, "An essay on Crimes and Punishment." London, 1788.

Buchholz, "Bettina." In *Deutsches Museum*, 1777², 231.

Bürger, G. A., "Sämmtliche Werke." Göttingen, 1829. I, 73, "Des armen Suschens Traum" (1773); I, 94f., "Neue weltliche hochdeutsche Reime, usw." (1773); I, 132, "Der Ritter und sein Liebchen" (1775); II, 160, "Hummel-Lied" (1789); II, 29, "Des Pfarrers Tochter von Taubenhain" (1781); II, 142, "Graf Walter (Nach dem Alt-Englischen)"; II, 213, "Der wohlgesinnte Liebhaber."

"G. A. Bürger in Göttingen und Gelliehausen." Karl Goedeke, Hannover, 1873. See especially p. 92f.

Cella, J. J., "Freymüthige Aufsätze." Anspach, 1784.

Claudius, Matthias, "Schönheit und Unschuld. Ein Sermon an die Mädchen." In "Sämmtliche Werke des Wandsbecker Boten." Gotha, 1882, I, 275.

"Commentatio succincta in Constitutionem Criminalem Caroli V. Imperatoris, etc." Hannover, 1736.

Cramer, C., "Der kluge Mann." Leipzig, 1801, Dritter Theil.

Falk, Franz, "Die Ehe am Ausgange des Mittelalters. Eine Kirchen- und Kultur-historische Studie." Freiburg im Breisgau, 1908.

Forster, Georg, "Sämmtliche Schriften." Herausgegeben von dessen Tochter und begleitet mit einer Charakteristik Forster's von G. G. Gervinus. Leipzig, 1843. II, "Johann Reinhold Forster's und Georg Forster's Reise um die Welt in den Jahren 1772 bis 1775." P. 101f.

"Oeuvres de Frédéric le Grand." Berlin, Decker, 1846–56. See especially IX, 30, "Dissertation sur les raisons d'etablir ou d'abroger les lois."

"Friedrich der Grosse." J. D. E. Preuss. Berlin, 1832.

Freisen, J., "Geschichte des Canonischen Eherechts bis zum Verfall der Glossenlitteratur." Tübingen, 1888.

Froitzheim, J., "Goethe und Heinrich Leopold Wagner, Ein Wort der Kritik an unsere Goethe-Forscher." Strassburg, 1889.

"Zu Strassburgs Sturm- und Drangperiode. 1770–1776." Strassburg, 1888.

Gemmingen, O. H. F. von, "Der deutsche Hausvater."
  First published in 1780. 1782 edition reprinted in
  "Deutsche Nationallitteratur," 139.
Geschichte und Erzählungen, Danzig, 1772–1778. II, 162,
  "Ein Brief über die herrschenden Laster unsers Zeital-
  ters."
Göckingk, L. F. G., "Jungfer Kamerohn und ihr Nachbar."
  In "Sinngedichte" p. 75. First published in *Taschen-
  buch für Dichter und Dichterfreunde*, I, 139.
Goethe, J. W., "Werke. Herausgegeben im Auftrage der
  Grossherzogin Sophie von Sachsen." Weimar, 1887–.
  I, I, 186, "Vor Gericht." Cf. *Idem*, p. 365.; I, 14,
  "Faust I." XXI, 67f., Wilhelm Meisters Lehrjahre.
"Der junge Goethe." Neue Ausgabe in sechs Bänden besorgt
  von Max Morris. Leipzig, 1910. II, 62, "Das Lied
  vom Herrn von Falkenstein"; II, 68, "Das Lied vom
  Herren und der Magd"; II, 80, "Das Lied vom braun
  Annel"; II, "Die Spinnerin."
"Goethe im Conseil. Urkundliches aus seiner amtlichen
  Thätigkeit 1778–1785." B. Suphan. In *Vierteljahr-
  schrift für Litteraturgeschichte*, Weimar, 1893, VI, 597.
Götz, J. N., "Klymene vor Gericht." In "Vermischte Ge-
  dichte." Hrsg. von K. W. Ramler, Mannheim, 1785,
  Pt. 3, 91.
Grimm, J., "Deutsche Rechtsalterthümer." Leipzig, 1889.
  See especially Vol. II.
Hebel, J. P., "Das heimliche Gericht." In "Werke" Deutsche
  Nationallitteratur, 142, part 2, 292.
Herder, J. G., "Ausgewählte Werke." In *Cotta'sche Bib-
  liothek der Weltliteratur*, II, 37, "Wiegenlied einer un-
  glücklichen Mutter"; II, 67, "O weh, o weh"; II, 198,
  "Klosterlied"; II, 301, "Für die Priesterehe." III,
  233f., Von den Vortheilen und Nachtheilen der heutigen
  Studiermethode."
Hess, Ludwig, von, "Freymüthige Gedanken über Staats-
  sachen." Hamburg, 1775.
Hippel, T. G., "Sämmtliche Werke." Berlin, 1828, V,
  "Ueber die Ehe" (1774); VI, "Ueber die bürgerliche

Verbesserung der Weiber" (1792); XI, "Ueber Gesetz-
gebung und Staatenwohl"; *Idem*, "Nachricht die von
K*sche Untersuchung betreffend. Ein Beitrag über
Verbrechen und Strafen" (1793).

Hermes, J. T., "Sophiens Reise von Memel nach Sachsen."
Leipzig, 1776, Vol. I, 620f.

Hamann, J. G., "Versuch einer Sibylle über die Ehe"
(1775). In "Schriften," Berlin, 1823, IV, 223f.

Hölty, L. H. C., "Gedichte," Königsberg und Leipzig, 1833.
I, 41, "Die Nonne"; I, 16, "Adelstan und Röschen."

Iselin, Isaak, "Gedanken über den Kindermord." In *Ephemeriden der Menschheit*, 1778, Viertes Stück. I was
unable to obtain this. Cf. *Allgemeine Deutsche Bibliothek*, 39, 588.

Jung-Stilling, "Heinrich Stillings Jugend und Jünglings-
jahre." In Bibliothek der deutschen Klassiker, IX.

Kant, I., "Sämmtliche Werke." Leipzig, 1867, IV, 159,
"Beantwortung der Frage; Was ist Aufklärung" (1784);
VII, 149, "Die Metaphysik der Sitten. Vom Straf-
und Begnadigungsrecht" (1797).

Katz, Edwin, "Ein Grundriss des kanonischen Strafrechts."
Berlin und Leipzig, 1881.

Keckeis, Gustav, "Dramaturgische Probleme im Sturm und
Drang." Bern, 1907.

Kindleben, C. W., "Studenten-Lexicon." Halle, 1781. In
"Bibliothek litterarischer und culturhistorischer Seltenheiten." Leipzig, 1899, No. 7.

Klinger, F. M., "Sämmtliche philosophische Romane."
Leipzig, 1810. I and II, "Fausts Leben, Thaten und
Höllenfahrt."

"Sämmtliche Werke." Stuttgart und Tübingen, 1842.
I and II, dramas, "Aristodemos," "Damokles."

Klippstein, see *Pfeil*.

Knapp, H., "Das alte Nürnberger Kriminalverfahren bis zur
Einführung der Carolina." München, 1892.

Köster, A., "Die allgemeinen Tendenzen der Geniebewegung
im 18. Jahrhundert."

Kreuzfeld, see *Pfeil*.

Lenz, J. M. R., "Gesammelte Schriften." Hrsg. von Ludwig Tieck, Berlin, 1828. I, "Der Hofmeister" and "Die Soldaten"; III, "Zerbin." The latter was published for the first time in *Deutsches Museum*, 1776[1], 116–131 and 193–207.

Lenz, J. M. R., "Ueber die Soldatenehen. Nach der Handschrift der Berliner Königlichen Bibliothek zum ersten Male herausgegeben von Karl Freye." Leipzig, 1914.

Laukhard, F. C., "Der Wild und Rheingraf Carl Magnus" (1798). Herausgegeben von Viktor Petersen, Stuttgart, 1911.

Leyser, "Meditationes ad pandectas." Ed. 3, IX, 698f.

List, G. D. K., "Ueber Hurerey und Kindermord." Mannheim, 1784.

Maurer, Konrad, "Ueber die Wasserweihe des germanischen Heidenthumes." München, 1880.

Meissner, A. G., "Lied einer Gefallenen." In *Deutsches Museum*, 1779[1], 379.

"Die Mörderin." In *Idem*, 1779[1], 380.

"Römische Annalen." In *Taschenbuch für Dichter und Dichterfreunde*, VI, 67. In *Idem*, IX, 15, "Das verliebte Bürgermädchen" (1778). *Idem*, X, 63, "Lied von der schwarzen Lise aus Kastilien."

"Ja wohl hat sie es nicht gethan!" (1795). In "Deutsche Litteraturdenkmale," 66/69, 71.

"Sammlung der Skizzen." Leipzig, 1796, IX, 350.

Meissner, C. F., "Zwo Abhandlungen über die Frage: Sind die Findel-Häuser vorteilhaft oder schädlich?" Göttingen, 1779.

Mendelssohn, Moses, "Gibt es natürliche Anlagen zum Laster?" In "Gesammelte Schriften," V, 678.

Miller, J. M., "Siegwart, Eine Klostergeschichte" (1775–1776). Stuttgart, 1844.

Montesquieu, C. L., "Spirit of laws translated from the French by Mr. Nugent." 3d ed., London, 1758.

Möser, Justus, "Sämmtliche Werke." Berlin, 1798. II, 163, "Ueber die zu unsern Zeiten verminderte Schande der Huren und Hurkinder"; IV, 118, "Ueber den Un-

terschied einer christlichen und bürgerlichen Ehe"; IV,
123, "Von den Militair-Ehen der Engländer"; VII, 208,
"Der Cölibat der Geistlichkeit von seiner politischen
Seite betrachtet"; IV, 130, "Ueber die Todesstrafen";
"Patriotische Phantasien," Berlin, 1842–43; V, 118,
"Von der Tortur"; V, 97, "Von einem Gebrauche zu
Pecking"; V, 107, "Also ist die Kirchenbusse so ganz
nicht abzuschaffen."

Müller, F. (Maler), "Das braune Fräulein." In "Stürmer
und Dränger." Hrsg. von A. Sauer. III, 266.

"Die Schaafschur" and "Das Nusskernen." In "Bibliothek der deutschen Klassiker," VIII, 696 and 720.

"Maler Müller." Bernhard Seuffert. Berlin, 1877.

Mylius, C., "Corpus Constitutionum Marchicarum, etc."

"Novum Corpus Constitutionum Prussico-Brandenbur-
gensium, etc." I was unable to obtain this, but it is important because it contains the decrees of Frederick the
Great. Cf. Preuss, J. D. E., "Friedrich der Grosse."
Berlin, 1832.

*Nassovia: Zeitschrift für nassauische Geschichte und Heimat-
kunde.* Wiesbaden, XIII, 249: Spielmann, C., "Kindesmord und seine Bestrafung im 17. Jahrhunderte"; IX,
146, Sandmann, E., "Peinliches Recht."

*Neue Bibliothek der schönen Wissenschaften und der freyen
Künste,* XXII, 75, contains an important review of Lenz's
"Zerbin."

Nicolai, C. F., "Politische und moralische Betrachtungen
über die Spartanische Gesetzgebung des Lykurgus."
In *Briefe die neueste Litteratur betreffend.* Berlin, 1765,
XXII, 129.

Pestalozzi, J. H., "Ueber Gesetzgebung und Kindermord.
Nachforschungen und Bilder. Wahrheiten und Träume.
Geschrieben 1780. Herausgegeben 1783." Frankfurt
und Leipzig. In "Sämtliche Werke." Hrsg. von L.
W. Seyffarth. Liegnitz, 1900, Vol. V.

Pfeffel, G. K., "Die Erkennung." In *Taschenbuch für Dichter
und Dichterfreunde,* IV, 116.

Pfeil, Klippstein and Kreuzfeld, "Drei Preisschriften über

die Frage: Welches sind die besten ausführbarsten
Mittel dem Kindermorde abzuhelfen, ohne die Unzucht
zu begünstigen?" Mannheim, 1784.

Der neue Pitaval. Eine Sammlung der interessantesten
Criminalgeschichten aller Länder aus älterer und neuerer
Zeit. Leipzig, 1857–1890. This contains a record of
many cases of infanticide committed in the seventeenth
and eighteenth centuries.

Runde, J. F., "Die Rechtmässigkeit der Todesstrafen aus
Grundsäzen des allgemeinen Staatsrechts vertheidigt."
In *Deutsches Museum,* 1777[1], 309.

Schummel, J. G., "Empfindsame Reisen durch Deutschland."
Wittenberg, 1770–1772.

Schiller, J. C. F., "Sämtliche Werke." Säkular-Ausgabe,
Stuttgart und Berlin, I, 30, "Die Kindesmörderin";
VIII, 222, "Die Polizei." For many imitations of
Schiller's poem see Erk-Böhme, "Deutscher Liederhort,"
I, 185.

Schink, J. F., "Empfindungen einer unglücklich Verführten."
Published in *Almanach der deutschen Musen,* 1777, 279.
I was not able to obtain this. Cf. Erich Schmidt, "Heinrich Leopold Wagner. Goethes Jugendgenosse," 1879,
p. 91.

Schlosser, J. G., "Die Wudbianer, Eine nicht gekrönte Preiss-
schrift über die Frage: Wie ist der Kindermord zu verhindern, ohne die Unzucht zu befördern?" Basel, 1785.
In "Kleine Schriften," IV.

Schlözer, A. L., *Briefwechsel.* Göttingen, 1780–1782.

Stats-Anzeigen, Göttingen, 1782–1793.

Schmidt, Erich, See *Wagner.*

Schmidt, K., "Wiegenlied einer unglücklichen Mutter."
In *Musenalmanach für 1787.* Voss und Gocking, p. 15.

Schubart, C. F. D., "Gesammelte Schriften." Stuttgart,
1839. VI, 145, "Beispiel einer altväterischen Tugend"
(1774), VI, 148, "Etwas Sonderbares" (1774).

"Das schwangere Mädchen." In "Stürmer und Dränger,"
III, 353.

"Gesammelte Schriften und Schicksale." Stuttgart, 1839,

IV, 147, "Minchen beim Grabe ihrer Mutter." IV, 330, "Lina an die Unschuld."

"Leben in seinen Briefen." Berlin, 1849.

"Hannchen an Wilhelm." In "Sämmtliche Gedichte." Stuttgart, 1842, II, 702.

Schweizer-Blatt, Zürich, 1782. Pestalozzi published parts of his essay on infanticide in this magazine. I was not able to obtain it.

"Single Life discouraged for the Publick Utility: or, an essay on Ways and Means for the Supplies of the Government." London, 1761.

Sonnenfels, J. v., "Grundsätze der Polizey, Handlung, und Finanzwissenschaft." München, 1787.

Spangenberg, Ernst, "David Georg Strube's Rechtliche Bedenken. Systematisch geordnet, ergänzt, berechtigt und mit Anmerkungen begleitet." Hannover, 1828, III, 31.

Sprickmann, A. M., "Das Neujahrsgeschenk. Eine Kloster-anekdote." In *Deutsches Museum*, 1776[2], 788; "Das Strumpfband, eine Klosterscene." In *Idem*, 1776[2], 1083; "Ida." In *Idem*, 1777[1], 120; "Horry. Eine tragische Scene." In *Idem*, 1778[1], 1; "Mariens Reden bei ihrer Trauung. Ein Fragment." In *Idem*, 1778[2], 232.

Stäudlin, G. F., "Die Missethäterin an ihren Säugling." In *Deutsche Nationalliteratur*, 135, 419f.

"Seltha, die Kindesmörderin." Published in *Schwäbisches Magazin für 1781*. I was not able to obtain this poem. Cf. Weltrich, R., "Friedrich Schiller." Stuttgart, 1885, p. 534.

Stelzer, C. J. L., "Christinchen" (1780). In *Taschenbuch für Dichter und Dichterfreunde*, II, 61.

Sturz, H. P., "Ueber Linguets Vertheidigung der Todesstra-fen" (1776). In "Bibliothek der deutschen Klassiker," VI, 709.

Stuve, R., "Nachrichten von der Frankfurtischen Garnison-schule; nebst Vorschlägen über die Soldatenehen." In *Berlinische Monatsschrift*, V, 213.

Sumner, W. G., "Folkways." Boston, 1907.

Süssmilch, J. P., "Die göttliche Ordnung in den Veränderungen des menschlichen Geschlechts." Berlin, 1761.

Thümmel, M. A. v., "Sämmtliche Werke." Leipzig, 1839, II, 1f.; VI, "Die Reise in die mittäglichen Provinzen von Frankreich." (1772–1791.)

Uz, J. P., "Die alten und die heutigen deutschen Sitten " in "Sämmtliche poetische Werke." Carlsruhe, 1776, II, 56.

Völkersamen, J., "Politische Vorschlag, dem Kindermord ohne alle Strafen und ohne dass der Fürst mit Erbauung eines Findelhauses beschwert werde, sicher vorzubeugen." See Erich Schmidt, "Heinrich Leopold Wagner." 1875, p. 60. I was not able to obtain this essay.

Wagner, H. L., "Die Kindermörderinn" (1776). In "Deutsche Litteraturdenkmale des 18. und 19. Jahrhunderts." Heilbronn, XIII.

"Heinrich Leopold Wagner. Goethes Jugendgenosse." Erich Schmidt, Jena, 1875, 2 ed., 1879.

Wehrli, Julius, "Der Kindsmord; dogmatisch-kritische Studie." Frauenfeld, 1889.

Wainlud, Samuel, "Die Kindestötung." Berlin, 1905.

Wilke, "Kindesmord bei Naturvölkern der Gegenwart und Vergangenheit." Braunschweig, 1898. In *Globus*, 74, No. 13, 211.

Willensbücher, Ferdinand, "Die strafrechtsphilosophischen Anschauungen Friedrichs des Grossen." Breslau, 1904.

Wilutzky, Paul, "Vorgeschichte des Rechts." Breslau, 1903, Vol. II.

Wucherer, W. F., "Julie oder die gerettete Kindsmörderinn " (1782). I was not able to obtain this production. Cf. Erich Schmidt, "Heinrich Leopold Wagner." 1875, p. 59.

Zander, F., "Unmut. An Minna." In *Musenalmanach*, 1779, Göttingen, bey Dietrich. This poem is ascribed to Bürger.

Zoepfl, Heinrich, "Die Peinliche Gerichtsordnung Kaiser Karl's V. nebst der Bamberger und der Brandenburger Halsgerichtsordnung." Heidelberg, 1842.

Zorn, J., "Die Motive der Sturm- and Drang Dramatiker, eine Untersuchung ihrer Herkunft und Entwicklung." Bonn, 1909.

INDEX.

VITA

Oscar Helmuth Werner was born in West Point, Nebraska, January 1, 1888. After completing the preparatory work at Enterprise Normal Academy, Enterprise, Kansas, and teaching one year in the public schools of Johnson County, Nebraska, he entered Central Wesleyan College in September, 1907. From this institution he was graduated in June, 1910, with the degree A.B. In June, 1908, Kansas Wesleyan University conferred on him the degree M. Accts. During the year 1910–11 he was Principal of the School of Business of his alma mater. The following year was spent at Northwestern University as Fellow in German. He was graduated from this institution in June, 1912, with the degree A.M. During the two following years he was Professor of German and French in Upper Iowa University. From September, 1914, to July, 1916, he was registered as a graduate student under the Faculty of Philosophy in Columbia University, devoting part of his time to the teaching of German in the department of Extension Teaching of the same University. Since September, 1916, he has been instructor in German in Case School of Applied Science.